GEORGE PASCHALIDIS

LOVE OPENING PATH TO LIFE

Media Vista Publications
ATHENS - GREECE

LOVE OPENING PATH TO LIFE
writer: GEORGE PASCHALIDIS

Copyright © George Paschalidis
Copyright © 2011

Media Vista Publications
9 Rimini str., 14231 Athens, Greece
Tel: +30 2117057088, Fax: +30 2117057598
www.mediavista.gr

ISBN: 978-960-9707-01-5

Desktop publishing: Excess Ltd,
47 Kolokotroni str., 105 60 Athens, Greece

I thank those who have supported me, stood by me and helped me. I would especially like to thank the volunteers for their invaluable assistance, the founding members of our Society for their trust, and those who played an important role at crucial junctures of my journey.
Among the many friends who have offered so much support, honorable mention should go to Lefteris Kapetanakis, George Chatzimichalis, Anda Matsinioti, Dimitri Georgelis, Eleni Asimakopoulou, Maria-Eleni Pantazi, Marianthi Gakoudi, Niki Gakoudi, Olga Atmatzidou, Panagiota Palioura, and Ilaira Kapetanaki for their support during the writing of this book.
I sincerely want to thank my good friend Paraskevi Salpisti Tornatorou for ensuring the intellectual property of this book.

CONTENTS

Premio Internazionale Giuseppe Sciacca

IX EDIZIONE 2010

TRE TARGHE D'ARGENTO E MEDAGLIA
del Presidente della Repubblica Italiana
MEDAGLIA
del Presidente della Camera dei Deputati

Si rilascia il Diploma a

Prot. n. /

Georgios Pashalidis
Premio Speciale Giuria per la Letteratura

Il Vice Presidente e Coordinatore Generale
Cav. Dott. Giovanni Cinque

Il Presidente del Premio
Rev. Prof. Bruno Lima

Il Segretario Generale
Avv. Francesco Saverio de Nardis

Città del Vaticano, 11.12.2010

FONDAZIONE ROMA
TERZO SETTORE

SIMAM
Servizi Industriali Manageriali Ambientali

Maccarinelli Cioff
L'EDIFICIO DIVENTA SOSTENIBILE

Ελληνική Εθνική Επιτροπή
για την UNESCO

Εκπαιδευτικός, Επιστημονικός
και Πολιτιστικός Οργανισμός των
Ηνωμένων Εθνών

ΟΜΙΛΟΣ ΓΙΑ ΤΗΝ UNESCO ΤΕΧΝΩΝ ΛΟΓΟΥ ΚΑΙ ΕΠΙΣΤΗΜΩΝ ΕΛΛΑΔΑΣ

ΕΠΑΙΝΟΣ

ΑΠΟΝΕΜΕΤΑΙ

Στον κ. *Γιώργο Πασχαλίδη*
για την προσφορά του στον άνθρωπο και την επιστήμη
και για την ανακάλυψη
των τριών ανθρωπίνων τύπων και του κυρίαρχου γονιδίου

ΑΘΗΝΑ, 31 ΜΑΡΤΙΟΥ, 2012

Υπό την αιγίδα της Ελληνικής Εθνικής Επιτροπής για την UNESCO

Ο ΠΡΟΕΔΡΟΣ   Ο ΓΕΝΙΚΟΣ ΓΡΑΜΜΑΤΕΑΣ

ΔΕΜΙΡΤΖΟΓΛΟΥ ΗΛΙΑΣ   **ΚΑΡΒΟΥΝΤΖΗΣ ΔΗΜΗΤΡΗΣ**

Preface

A few words about the author, George Paschalidis

"What you emit is what you have.
What you give is what you receive"

When we were young children, we loved to discover new things. The search itself gave us joy and when we actually happened to come across a "treasure", our joy was overwhelming. We would then run to our friends with a burning desire to share it with them. How important, accepted and unique it made us feel!

This act of sharing at such a young age was for many of us an important aspect in our self-realization. The feeling that we could enlighten our friends, as well as bask in the glory of their reaction, raised our self-esteem.

The explanation for these feelings only came later, when we grew up. This explanation lies behind the very etymology of the Greek word for "information" (pliroforia), which means "to effect completion".

It is these feelings that we experience when sharing with you the valuable information that follows.

Today, something extraordinary has taken place in Greece. *There is a fellow human being who has been gifted with the* **power of healing and the knowledge of the link between the Visible and the Invisible, the Cause and the Effect.**

Initially people used to meet George (as he encourages us to call him) in Alexandria, a town in the Greek prefecture of Imathia. Now they can meet him in Thessalonica and in Athens, where he spends a few days every month. Many other Europeans also have the opportunity to meet him, as he often travels to Europe to meet and help doctors and patients who ask for his assistance and knowledge.

When you first meet George Paschalidis, you are impressed with his modesty, his unselfishness, his smile and his jubilant mood. The love he feels for mankind is enormous and clearly evident.

He has the ability to intuitively evaluate the overall state of health of the human body using a scale he devised himself, according to which 1 signifies perfect health and 100 the total lack of it. These indicators represent the hormonal disorder of the body, i.e. the existence or non-existence of a disorder caused by the lack of balance between the hormones and the nervous system. The higher this disorder indicator is, the more acute the resulting disease is for the body.

George Paschalidis has also classified people into **three types,** depending on their skeletal structure. Each type has its own **characteristics** and **sensitivities**, which are analyzed extensively in the chapters of this book.

Once he has "seen" the disorders of the human body, he intervenes immediately and effectively with a kind of healing **energy**, thus helping to restore health.

However, the most important contribution George Paschalidis has made is the fact that **he knows and explains in detail the process that causes illnesses.** That is, the ways of life that, as they clash with the temperament of each human type, cause the body to exhibit a disease.

In other words, George Paschalidis presents to us our "structural pattern" a "detailed user guide" of our body. He gives us **instructions for our benefit**.

It is worth noting that this important piece of work has been carried out without pressure or anxiety, since George himself is direct, amiable and disarmingly natural in his speech and demeanor. Those who have met George Paschalidis share the impression that his warmth and care is that of a father to his children. His advice is a seed that needs our involvement in order to sprout. The grief and problems he encounters in his everyday contact with people are so great that they would discourage even the bravest of men. However, he is so insatiably optimistic and so filled with genuine joy that he sweeps you up and often makes you laugh to tears. He penetrates the complex, goes to the heart of the problem and finds the deeper causes of the illness.

When he speaks to the public, he touches upon subjects that concern attitudes to life in general. In this way, he makes us observe and reflect upon aspects of our individual personality. To our astonishment, we recognize that attitudes and behaviors that were either inexplicable to us or went unnoticed can now be explained. At the same time, we realize how these attitudes and behaviors have impacted the people closest to us.

He always addresses the public, trying in a subtle

and discreet manner to focus on and analyze particular situations an individual may encounter. By presenting the problem to the public, he helps individuals to gain an increased awareness of the problems they generally encounter in their lives.

He brings out deep, hidden sentiments that, as soon as they come to the surface, relieve the sufferer and at the same time teach the observer the power of the truth.

One is struck with this expression of love with which he embraces each person prior to the diagnosis or the therapy. His ability to give pure, unconditional love is an exceptionally difficult and arduous task.

George Paschalidis' advice is given according to one's type, way of life, weaknesses or personal problems he/she may be confronted with. He explains our personal abilities, often blocked by ourselves, and he analyzes the ways in which we may unblock ourselves and overcome our problems.

"We should open our hearts, because we all have love deep inside, in some remote obscure corner, tucked away and frozen beneath our thoughts and our musts", he urges those who seek his advice.

The more we approach him, the more we understand his effort to reach out and touch people deeply, so that they themselves will eventually be empowered to reflect on their lives and become more complete and true to themselves. He shows us how easy it is to take hold of our lives, to understand that we ourselves can change the course of our life, learn how to live and enjoy every single day, without worrying about tomorrow and without being stuck in the past.

George Paschalidis' gift to us is not only the relief or healing on a physical level, but also the opportunity he offers us to find a better balance with ourselves; to see our life in a new perspective. What is essential is not only that we recuperate; the most important thing is to recognize and eventually remove the obstacles from our life.

His endurance and energy never cease to impress us. He remains inexhaustible, boundless and cheerful throughout the entire day. He is an inspiration to all the volunteers by the vitality he exudes and they in turn, filled his vitality, infuse with energy the people who come to receive his help or just to listen to what he has to say.

The joy, the intensity of emotion and the sense of completion that arise at the end of his diagnosis of the causes of one's illnesses and problems always astound us and sweep us up in this inundation of Love.

George Paschalidis has received the gift of immediate access to knowledge and lives the life of harmony. He shares with us this knowledge and he shows us its source, which is love, encouraging us all to enter into the sphere of harmony.

He never ceases to urge us: *"If you only knew how easy it is! It only takes a click!"*

This book deals with the life and work of George Paschalidis. It aims is to propagate his work. We all hope that one day science will benefit from his knowledge and will use it to offer relief to people.

We feel particularly privileged that we have been among the first to have had the opportunity to taste this ultimate joy of learning.

George Paschalidis' work is difficult; perhaps arduous for our earthly body. It is also equally difficult for the scientists who will attempt to convey his scientific knowledge, for they will surely have to surpass themselves.

We wish them strength and success.

In concluding this preface, we thank George Paschalidis for the love he has shown us by inviting us to participate in his noble effort. We were beside him when he was writing this book and have experienced the exuberance all meetings with him have. It is the kind of joy and security we used to feel when our parents took us to visit our favorite relatives. We were with him when his work and life were transferred onto paper, leaving us with this small concern: What about Love? Will it be possible to convey it on paper?

The friends of George and his work

George Paschalidis narrates

My life before and after the Power

I was born in Aiginion, in the Greek prefecture of Pieria, of humble parents, whom I loved and will always love. Like all people I spent my early years in Aiginion playing with my brother and friends.

I only finished primary school and I was awarded a grade 7 out of 10. From the age of twelve to fifteen, I worked as a carpenter in a workshop making furniture. During the next two years, I worked as a welder in a garage. From the age of seventeen to twenty, I served in the army as an excavator driver. I briefly returned to the furniture workshop and at the same time I distributed blood donation pamphlets. For the next two years, I worked again as an excavator driver, in Serres and in Thessalonica. At the age of twenty-three I was hired by a contractor who worked in Libya in Ubari, Sabha, Edri and Ghat. I lived in these towns, in the Sahara Desert, for three years. After I returned to Greece, I worked as a farmer and married the woman of my life, my wife Chrysoula, with whom I have two children, Dimitris and Eleftheria, who have stood me in my efforts, and I thank them for this.

Next, I ran my wife's family business, a restaurant in Alexandria, a town in the northern Greek prefecture of Imathia.

I have never been shy about undertaking new ventures and new challenges whenever I saw the opportunity to test my talents and new skills.

My job at the tavern proved to be good practice for my patience and perseverance; a testing ground that taught me to serve people and offer them both material and spiritual food to satify their needs.

An excursion to Olympus

In 2002, some time before Easter, I was with my son and my friends, Pericles and Apostolis, at the foot of Mt. Olympus. All of a sudden, I felt the urgency to dig at a particular spot. I did so, and immediately water sprang out and started to flow from that spot. The more I dug, the more water gushed out and with greater volume. I was stunned. At the same time, I felt something changing in me. I began to "see", to perceive beyond and further than what normal human sight allows. The newly found sense scared me because, among other things, I had never sought it, nor had I ever thought about such transcendental issues.

Four months later, again with the same friends, we climbed Mt. Olympus where, near a brook, I felt an electromagnetic band permeate my head; it felt as if I had been struck by lightning. Its power was so great and sudden that I felt that my head was going to split into two. The pain was unbearable. I got skin burns wherever metal, such as my watch or my bracelet, touched my body. At the same time, I experienced a newly-felt change in my head, as if it vibrated differently now. The shock was so great that the only thing I wanted was to leave the place without any further delay. I was carried home by my friend, Theofanis; I was exhausted. The pains in my head continued for two whole months.

Five months later, I was in Ano Seli with five friends.

Once again, I felt this sudden pain; the energy waves were running through me again, only even stronger this time. This process lasted for almost four hours. The feeling was so intense that my friend Vangelis stood there staring at me, speechless. He did not dare to talk to me or touch me; he only kept staring and observing my reactions.

A few days after this incident, I was at a small church by the Aliakmon River with Theofanis, Pericles and Apostolis. Once again, I felt a sudden, acute pain at the upper part of my forehead which made me feel as if my head was splitting in two. My body began to convulse under the influence of a mysterious force. The whole experience this time was even more intense than the previous time.

My friend, Pericles, who was standing closest to me, saw my convulsions and tried to support me once more. I passed out, but my whole body was still shaking. He slapped me and threw some cold water on my face to help me regain my senses. "You had it coming!" he joked about it later. I thanked him wholeheartedly for standing by me throughout this painful experience of my transformation. He still supports, as all the other friends from that period of my life have done: Makis, who opened the way to me, and Giannis, who helped me progress in it.

Five months later, following a visit to a monastery, I felt a pressure on my head, with acute pains that lasted for some four hours. And then, a novel experience dawned on me: now I could feel and "see" a continuous flow of light waves permeating my right hand and radiating outward. At that moment, I realized that all the energy I had been receiving was now under my control and I could direct it and emit it.

All these unexpected events took place every four months within a two-year time span (2002 to 2004). They happened a total of seven times. After the last time, I began to receive the Knowledge. Whatever question I asked myself, I had the answer. Even questions that had never crossed my mind were revealed to me. My initial reaction after the shock was to feel scared, then came fear of the unknown, and eventually the whole experience developed into a game. For example, friends would phone me from their house or places I had never visited and I would describe to them the environment around them, their exact location, their posture at that moment, how many people they were with and who these people were. This game helped me keep my emotional balance.

At a certain moment, I was asked for something that had never crossed my mind. The answer I gave almost automatically, when crossed-checked against the facts, proved to be the correct one. After this latest incident, I realized to my surprise that whatever question was put to me, at home, while with friends, in the tavern, the answer was formed in my mind. Whatever the question I posed to myself, there came the answer! It is like a radar emitting waves that return bringing with them the desired information. When I ask myself the question of transfer in time, I can "see" how transfer can be achieved. Time and space travel, after all, is a question of mind over matter.

Some time passed during which I realized that I possessed some unique powers, which I had not yet figured out how to manage. I felt alone; I was scared.

At this point in time, Easter 2003, a friend who knew what was happening to me, asked me to try and help her nephew. It was the first time that I was asked to deal with a health problem ailing a fellow human being.

This young man, the nephew of the friend, was suffering from some serious sort of psoriasis. Besides the treatments using orthodox medicine, he had also tried all sorts of alternative cures, but to no avail. Finally, he visited me along with his aunt at the tavern in Alexandria. He was a young man whose body was completely covered in a strange membrane like a "crust". He stood in front of me. I immediately saw that he could be cured, and very quickly. I was scared at the realization that this boy could be cured without me even touching him and without any medical treatment.

Later, his aunt would narrate the story of his cure: "His entire body and face was just like the trunk of an old tree. The third day after the therapy, his mother called me to inform me that his bed sheets were covered with dry pieces of skin that fell off his body; he was now clean. Within three weeks, he was in a perfectly normal condition."

The boy was exhilarated. "Now, after the cure, I am so happy; I dress as I like, I go out, I live as I want, and all this is due to Mr. George."

The shock I felt with the cure of this young man, who is now always beside me, cleared of his psoriasis, was great. I found myself in unknown territory, in possession of powers whose extent I did not know, nor did I know what to do with them, what to do with my life, or where this path would take me. Only if someone could put himself in my shoes would they understand how perplexed I was!

The second case was introduced to me by the same friend. She asked me to do something about a friend of hers, a young girl who was bedridden since the age of two and half. It was then that I realized I could cure somebody by phone from a distance. The young girl got up from the bed and walked.

I was an ordinary man, an everyday guy like all of us, and all of a sudden I was "chosen" to be the recipient of a power that exceeds the limits of mind and imagination.

Gradually, many people started to come to me and ask for my help and advice on all kinds of diseases. Our tavern in Alexandria was transformed into a reception hall for people.

I had not yet discovered the knowledge of the human body, its structure and function. I simply used to wonder about something and as soon as I asked myself a question, then all would seem familiar. So, I began to enquire about everything with respect to the functioning of the body and my answers, as I cross-checked them with the facts later, were spot on. I would "see" (i.e. identify) the problem or disorder in the body, and after a medical examination it would appear that my "diagnosis" was correct; I had "seen" the right answer.

I became aware that some great power was given to me, as well as a higher diagnostic ability; I was stunned by the realization. Initially it scared me, unknown as it were, but at the same time I was carried away with the joy of discovery. The fact that I could "see" filled me with enthusiasm and I carried on as if it was a game. I would say that playing this "game" got me where I am now. I tried my best never to be left alone, to always be among other people, so that I wouldn't think about the unknown path opening in front of me.

I was constantly discovering that the answers I would give were confirmed by science, through unassailable scientific tests. People I had never seen before in my life, for whom I would make a diagnosis or analysis, would subsequently go to medical laboratories and find out that the findings of the scientific analyses were exactly as I had described them myself.

It is easy to write down these experiences, and even easier to read them as a story. It is, however, impossible for one to comprehend the magnitude of the spiritual, emotional and physical strength required to go through them.

It is so easy to "see", but at the same time so difficult to live among the people that you "see". In order to do this effectively, one must function with just one emotion and that is total Love. Only then can you become one with people. If you function based on emotions, because they change with thought, which in turn changes with the speed of light, you obtain your emotions you go through in life and distance yourself from other people and enclose yourself in solitude and grief. When solitude prevails, however, then one cuts themselves off from Love. Even Heaven is made for two.

Gandhi had once said that there is enough on earth for everybody's need; however people's greed is so great that it can never be fulfilled. In the process, my ambition and my greed were both tested; the few that attempted to exploit me soon failed. I denied everything and thus I gained everything.

What I ask from those close to me is that, if they happen to get tired, or are influenced by others, or have their own reasons to give up, they should know that I love them, and that the only thing I would wish would be that they leave quietly, so as not to cause any harm to themselves. They cannot hinder my work, for it has already been set in motion.

An opening abroad

In October, 2004, and while people from all around Greece had started to flock to Alexandria, there came a Greek that was employed in Dr Peter Mandel's clinic in Bruchsal, Germany. They had been informed of my special powers and invited me to visit them. The first trip was scheduled for the following month, while in the meantime I had already helped the doctor himself with paralysis of his right foot he had had for over five years. At the same time, I had also helped a lady colleague of his. This young lady was about to get married. She had undergone medical examinations that showed a problem of malignity on her breast. She was desperate about it. "My gift for your wedding", I told her, "will be revealed to you on the Monday after your wedding. You will repeat your medical examinations and this time, they will be negative." And so they were.

Dr Peter Mandel was internationally acclaimed for his discovery of the so-called Diagnosis of Terminal Energy Points (ETD), a method that is similar and complementary to existing traditional medical examinations. ETD provides doctors with information of very high diagnostic accuracy and it concurs with clinical findings 75% - 87.5% of the time.

Dr Mandel played a significant role in my development during that period, because he offered me, through the use of his equipment, the possibility to test and confirm the accuracy of my power of diagnosis and therapy, and to prove the accuracy of my human typology.

Several patients of his clinic were examined and I was also asked to offer my own diagnosis of their condition. My diagnosis was then compared with the medical examinations of the patients and also with further examinations that took place following my healing intervention.

At this point, I would like to mention the case of a German lady who visited Dr Mandel's clinic. This lady had just received the results of her medical tests, which, of course, I was unaware of. As soon as I saw her, I diagnosed that she suffered from hepatitis C. When Dr Mandel learned about my diagnosis he was surprised, but at the same time he felt happy and vindicated for having invited me, as this invitation had already bore its first fruit.

Fifteen minutes after my "energy" intervention (therapy), her tests were repeated on the same equipment. The doctors declared that all the readings had returned to normal levels.

The shock was great and naturally very pleasing for the patient. It was even greater for me, as well as for the German doctors. They kept calling their colleagues to come and compare the different results of the two tests of the patient, which had taken place within just twenty minutes!

The second patient was showing symptoms of a stroke. I asked myself what could be the cause of this condition. Through a process of questions and answers, I came to the conclusion that his skeletal structure was to blame. I observed a slight congenital cervical lesion, which caused a malfunction of his circulatory system that resulted in the stroke. At that time, in the adjacent ward, there was another patient that had suffered a cardiac arrest. I was pondering on the causes of his condition and I observed that also in his case there was a slight lesion on the cervical spine at a different spot this time. I realized then that this lesion had increased the pressure on the central artery, which resulted in the cardiac arrest.

I wondered then, whether there is some kind of categorization of humans in terms of their skeletal structure and immediately I realized that *there are only three skeletal types for all humanity.*

The shock, the feeling of responsibility and my anxiety as to how I should manage all this new knowledge were so intense that I withdrew into myself. I was trying to collect data in order to make this information comprehensible to people and, mainly, to be able to convey it to the medical community.

For the next four days and for twenty-four hours a day, Dr Mandel's medical practice was flocked with dozens of patients, all of them receiving accurate diagnoses and spectacular cures. The enthusiasm of the doctors that were present to check the diagnoses and the cures, was, I believe, even higher than that of the patients. The whole process had resulted in my permanent collaboration with Dr Mandel in numerous clinics and practices in many other countries, including Italy, Switzerland, Austria and Spain, where new avenues were opened in my itinerary.

During my stay in Germany, as I saw the patients and diagnosed their health problems, I tried to classify them in terms of a scale that I had invented myself – arbitrary at this stage – in order to facilitate my readings of the data and also to have an easier and more efficient collaboration with the doctors. The scale ranged from 1 to 100. I wanted to see at which point on the scale the human body begins to present health problems. I noticed that as the index on the scale climbed higher, the more serious the health problem was (at point 64, e.g., the diagnosis shows cancer). The scale index, combined with increased stress, revealed explosive reactions in the behavior of the patients, due to their psychological condition. I called the index of the total hormonal function "Total Hormonal Disorder". The pivotal question of the existence and consequences of the "Total Hormonal Disorder" is analyzed in the relevantly titled chapter of this book.

The disorder that I speak about concerns and quantifies the consequences that the psychological disorder (nervousness, anxiety, intense sorrow etc.) has on the body and the disorders it can cause to the human body. Psychological and physical conditions are related to one another; they absolutely depend on each other. **All diseases are psychosomatic.** None is exclusively due to purely psychological or biological factors, unless its occurrence is caused by contamination from elements in the environment (like radiation or asbestos), or genetically inherited.

In one of these trips, I attended a conference in Italy with Dr Mandel. The conference was about orthodox and alternative medicine. At the conference, I was asked to undergo a measurement of my healing power at the International Institute of Biophysics in Noyce, Germany. The Director of the Institute, Prof. Fritz-Albert Popp, measures the emission of photons from the hands of healers with the help of equipment that he has developed. After the results of the measurements, that left the doctors stunned, I was finally absolutely certain about myself!

However, this situation had started to cause me some apprehension, as I was concerned that people approaching me were intending to take advantage of my knowledge for their own benefit. That made me distance myself from the individual, and now I am amongst many people. I feel more secure this way. My aim is not the welfare of one, but of everyone, and to change everyone's way of life. This, after all, is the primary concern of the book you are holding in your hands.

After Germany, I returned to Alexandria so certain of myself that ever since, I have devoted myself to this purpose. In Greece, however, there is not much room for collaboration. It is very difficult for scientists to accept this knowledge or for research institutions to facilitate this much-needed research. However, as a human being and as a Greek, I have decided, before I leave the country and move on, to conclude a cycle of service to my homeland.

An opening in Greece

For the reasons above, I decided to organize meetings in five cities in Greece. A former patient of mine named O, who had been cured in Alexandria of a serious ailment, offered to help me organize some meetings in Chalkida. So for two days, I stayed in a hotel that provided me with a conference hall. For the next two days, dozens of people came to see me. The results were impressive.

The second destination was Athens, since people were expecting me there too. The first meetings took place at a house of a lady that had once come to see me in Alexandria for health reasons and offered to help me with my work.

These two ladies contributed to the changing of my course, so that finally I remained in Greece.

In Athens, many patients started to visit me and received my help. Many doctors also expressed a keen interest in the research aspect of my healing.

The vast influx of visitors led us to move to larger premises in Athens. At the same time... At the same time, another reception centre was opened in Thessalonica to house meetings and discussions.

There have been people who approached me with the purpose of using the Knowledge accorded to me for their own benefit, be it their self-promotion or financial gain. However, the work is done on a non-profit basis, and does not leave room for personal ambitions. All of these people resigned from their efforts and left empty-handed, thus depriving themselves of the joy of being part of what is taking place at these meetings.

With the start of the functioning of our Foundation, in Pylea, Thessalonica, the cycle that started in Alexandria in 2002 had reached its conclusion. Many residents of Pylea had stood by me and did their utmost to keep me with them. However, life moves on and we have to do the same; we must follow its path.

I do not feel that I have left the people of Alexandria. I am near them, and I love them. They supported me so that I can be what I am now; they embraced me with love and still stand by me to this day.

I also want to thank everybody at my birthplace, my relatives, the local people and my neighbors, and all those who have stood by me. I love them and I am grateful to them.

In the process, many people in Greece and abroad have offered to help as volunteers; men and women willing to participate in this spreading of the communion of love and joy. Their help is invaluable.

The path to Knowledge

Man and the World

Man develops spiritually when he follows a path of self-knowledge and a knowledge of those around him. The self, that is we ourselves, is not only our thoughts but also our emotions, our preferences, our instincts, our actions and decisions, our relationships with those around us and nature at large and our choices.

Since the dawn of human history, we have devoted a great part of our activities to the research and exploration of the self, on the ways we interact and relate to one another and the environment in general, our wonderful planet, the Universe of the Creation and the Creator Himself.

At the Temple of the Oracles in Delphi, the most sacred site in ancient Greece, an inscription summons people to "Know Thyself", that is to pursue self-knowledge. It is an exhortation to know oneself. This adage is attributed to Apollo, the god of the Sun, who bequeathed light to humanity.

However, only the Biblical command, "Increase you and multiply", given by the Lord to Man, condenses and defines so accurately the purpose of our existence on Earth, and *reveals the Creator's plan for His most perfect creation.*

In order to "increase", you must have self-knowledge and broaden your understanding of your place in the world. It is plain that this ought to be our primary maxim. The good Lord has sown our species on this earth so that we develop spiritually ("increase you"), with the ultimate aim to meet Him come the day, and at the same time to reproduce ("multiply"), in order to populate the Earth and flourish, using wisely whatever the Earth has to offer us, never forgetting that *we are* part of it.

Sadly, with the passing of time, we people have forgotten our divine origin, tamed the spark of our minds and limited ourselves by giving divine status to science.

We forgot that *we are part of a whole*. We neglected to see that *we are also one entity comprised of Mind, Body and Spirit*. The state of today's society seems to be a result of this oblivion. Many intellectuals and thinkers, both past and present, profess that we did not fare so well in keeping ourselves up to the level of the purpose of our existence.

The world of science

In the effort to come to know ourselves and our nature, we developed science and technology, enjoying their benefits but without considering their consequences. Yet it always seems that something is missing either at the level of knowledge, or at the level of understanding, or the way we perceive it as a whole.

Social science, which includes among other disciplines history, sociology, psychology, anthropology, law and political science, is the study and regulation of the human behavior. It views people, with various degrees of success, both as an individual and as a member of a specific society at a particular

time. And, whilst it offers numerous theories that are of interest to each disciplihe, none of them has so far managed to provide solutions to the impasses reached by contemporary man. Even psychology, which a lot of people had at one time hoped could given the answer to everything, proved to be...
"Psycho-logy (talking about the psyche), yes, but leaving the Psyche, the Soul, untouched..."

The positive and natural sciences, such as mathematics, computer science, physics and chemistry, after centuries of efforts to trying to understand the "world order", now acknowledge that what they know, even if valid, only represents a small aspect of what is happening around us and that even this is unknown to them. Beyond the three dimensions of space (height, width and depth) that are familiar to us, and even beyond the dimension of time, which is always present, scientists have discovered that the laws governing the microcosm (whatever exists in the atom, within the cell) and the macrocosm (the universe, the planets) are different.

Matter, according to contemporary scientific knowledge, is not something concrete, as we perceive it to be. Matter is, at its core, energy and light that pulsate. Everything in the universe is light and electricity: pure energy.

Summarily speaking, in school we learn that the atom looks like a sphere with another sphere inside it called the nucleus and electrons rotate around the nucleus, just like the planets around the sun. Today, scientists find this model oversimplified and describe the atom like a small nebula, a cloud, that pulsates with light and energy.

During the last fifty years, these new ideas and findings have led to the formulation of yet another novel theory of the nature of things that is now widely accepted among the scientific community. This is the so-called 'Unified Theory'. According to this theory, the part is contained in the whole, everything is contained in something else and nothing in the Universe exists in itself. Modern physical science, moreover, maintains that all people and all things are comprised of the same molecules from which Creation was started and biology reminds us that in our genes we carry bits of our earliest ancestors, but not just them.

Naturally, you may wonder why science took so many centuries and such painstaking effort to discover what is instinctively known to most of us; a knowledge that exists in most cultures, in all traditions and mythologies that everything is interconnected, even if they appear unrelated or totally different. It is also known that most scientific disciplines deal with knowledge of the individual and avoid stydying the whole, the universal.

Yet, in reality, after so many generations of conflict among the sciences, it is now acknowledged that there is a need for a unified, total reality that embraces us all, appeases us with its existence and deeply relieves us. And the reason that this is happening today around us and why such theories are being advanced is the fact that man is seeking a new morality, a new spirituality, one that demands that we put aside our individualism and open ourselves up to Love.

Humanity has reached the point of progress which dictates that it is now imperative to develop the asset of selfless love, unconditional love, in order to continuously advance. We all suspect and we all have a feel that it is not possible to continue further without love.

"We should open our hearts because we all have love deep inside, in some remote obscure corner, tucked away and frozen beneath our thoughts and our musts."

Now is the moment for the seed of Love which is hidden in all of us to sprout. We all feel this when, frustrated with what may be presented to us as a realistic picture of present-day humanity, we withdraw in ourselves and seek refuge in the knowledge of our cell, the awareness of our depth. It is this type of pressure exerted by the seed against the soil when it begins to sprout. The heart swells and the mind cannot explain this. Nature itself calls us to open up our heart for love to reveal itself; the love that we have induced into hibernation.

It is the mind that struggles and fights off the heart. The latter wants to let love overflow. This internal conflict disturbs us, creates an unsettling feeling, prevents us from realizing that everything originates in the mind of the Lord, and it all exist within Him, interwoven into a magnificent woof of Harmony.

We insist on existing, forgetting that in reality we have no other option but to co-exist, since it is the Cosmic Law that commands us to live together.

"We say 'exist', but the correct approach is to 'co-exist', for it is not possible to exist alone'.

Categories / Types of human personality

From the moment man began to contemplate the concept of personality and to observe himself and others, he attempted to systematize the differences and similarities between his fellow men by applying a system of classification similar to that he used in order to understand and classify natural phenomena.

Some people, therefore, collated and classified the observations they had made themselves, as well as those of others, with the aim of arriving at more general conclusions regarding man and his characteristics. This process, which is so popular at times when everything was viewed in a mechanistic spirit and which – in the hands and the minds of some people – became such an enormous distortion, has a long history. This effort, the articulation of a representative typology of man, continues unabated to the present day. It is worth noting that, although most people start from a different starting point, they arrive at the same conclusions. However, in modern science, as well as in psychology, categorizations of this kind are considered greatly incomplete and vague, and thus are to be avoided.

Below we quote some attempts at categorization known since ancient times. We will also present a more recent one.

Hippocrates

Hippocrates (460-377 BC), a doctor from the Greek island of Kos, is considered to be the Father of medical science. He showed interest in human features and he formulated a typology that is based on the balance and proportion of the liquid components in the human body. Having studied the sources available to him and having classified the information he had collected, he based his theory on Empedocles' (circa 494-434 BC) human philosophy to formulate his theory of the four fluids.

The great philosopher Empedocles maintained that there are two principles that govern the world: 'friendship' ('philotes') and 'strife' ('neikos'). These two principles strive to control the four natural elements ('rizomata') that form the world: fire, air, water and earth.

Hippocrates, reflecting Empedocles' theory for the world and the human body, formulated the idea that human health depends on four fluids, or liquid substances, that exist in the human body. These are the "blood" (created in the veins), the "phlegm" (the mucous or the lymphatic system, created in the liver), the yellow bile (related to the cyst) and the black bile, (a product of processes occuring in the spleen). These elements have some specific qualities, to the effect that their correct proportion and balance in the body defines its overall balance.

Correlating this to George Paschalidis' typology, described below, we may make the following connections:

Blood corresponds to the human type **A**

Phlegm corresponds to the human type **B**

Yellow and black bile correspond to

the human type **C**

Also, according to Hippocrates, nature consists of four elements (earth, water, air and fire) that he believed influence human behavior. This observation by Hippocrates is considered as the first time that human behavior has been attributed to biological causes.

Again, in correlation to George Paschalidis' typology, these elements refer to:

Air to the human type **A**

Water to the human type **B**
Fire to the human type **C**

It should be noted that the earth is not considered an individual element by Hippocrates because it is composed of a synthesis of air, water and fire.

Galen

Galen (128-200AD) was a Greek doctor from Pergamus whose theories greatly influenced medical science during the medieval period. He developed his own typology based on Hippocrates. Galen linked the four fluids of Hippocrates with the existence of the four personality types.

According to Galen, then, there are:
The Blood-based type: lively, emotionally unstable (dominated by blood)
The Phlegmatic-type: detached, distant (dominated by phlegm)
The Bile type: quick tempered, emotionally stable (dominated by the yellow bile)
The Melancholic type: unhappy, lethargic, isolated (dominated by the dark bile)

Matching these with the typology of George Paschalidis we have:

Blood type: Human Type **A**

Phlegmatic type: Human type **B**

Bile or Cholic - mournful type: Human type **C**

Plutarch

According to the historian and philosopher Plutarch (circa 50 – 120 A.D.) men are distinguished by three types:

Practical: Type **A** according to
George Paschalidis' typology

Theoretical: Type **B** according to
George Paschalidis' typology

Physical: Type **C** according to
George Paschalidis' typology

Plato

The great philosopher Plato (427-347 BC) maintained that the ideal polity should include three types of men.

Rulers (governors) – type **A** according to
George Paschalidis' typology

Soldiers (who are concerned with security) –
type **B** according to George Paschalidis' typology

Laborers (who provide all necessary goods and services) – type **C** according to George Paschalidis' typology

Ayurveda*

Ayurveda, the most ancient of all therapeutic systems which originated in India and has a history that goes back 4000 years also has classified people into three distinct categories.

The three ayurverdic types:
The airy type (Vata)

The main feature that marks the airy type is *mobility* and *flexibility*. The physical and mental world of this psychosomatic type is in constant flux. Just like air is constantly in motion, the Vata person is always on the move, disorganized, spontaneous and creative. They cannot keep a schedule for their life. They are "artistic" and "bohemian" types. They have many ideas and in general are considered by others to be "clever", quick and dynamic.

(The data that refer to the three human types according to Ayurveda were provided by my dear friend Mr. Andreas Tsourouktsoglou, a neurologist and psychiatrist and director of the Therapeutic Laser Unit in a large medical center of Athens. He is also scientific director of Homeopathic Medicine and the

The way the Vata person describes things is characterized by *disarray*; the topic of the discussion shifts quickly, following every new thought that occurs in their mind. New ideas spring up inadvertently all the time. They always follow them and, as a result, their train of thought is derailed. They have a weak memory. They get angry easily, shout if upset, but calm down quickly and forget it.

They often suffer from headaches and migraines caused by stress; They have breathing problems and are out of breath, have tachycardia and palpitations or arrhythmias, flatulence and bowel movement problems. Vata women have menstrual cycle problems. Their joints appear to be dry (let's not forget that air dries humidity) and may make a characteristic cracking sound, especially the knee joints when walking or the neck joints when turning the head. This type is sensitive to neurological problems and may develop multiple sclerosis, epilepsy or senility more often than other people.

System of Ayurveda for the Online Encyclopedia of Medicine and author of the book, Ayurveda – The Science of Life, ed. Ayurveda Hellas. I thank him warmly.)

Watery / earthy type (Kapha)

The main characteristic of the watery nature is *sluggishness* and *slowness*. The way they speak is sluggish, slow, reserved. think a lot before they talk. They are what we would call "the typical emotional person". They are very shy. They never offer many details about their problems, but if asked, they remember a lot regarding their health and life in general. They sit calmly, do not move much and do not seem to be perturbed easily when talking about their health.

The health problems of a Kapha type mainly concern edema and swelling. Because their metabolism is slow, they tend to gain weight easily and lose it with difficulty and they show increased levels of cholesterol, triglycerides and lipids. They suffer from indigestion and bloating in the stomach. Kapha women tend to retain water and as a result they suffer from bloating in the stomach, chest and even face.

They often suffers from bronchial problems, colds in winter and increased catarrh (runny nose) and production of mucous. They also suffer from allergic rhinitis (rhinorrhea).

Watery types are overweight, with an increased tendency of obesity and retention of liquids. They also tend to develop thyroid nodules, cysts in the chest, fibroids (myomata) in the womb, cysts in the ovaries etc. They also have a tendency to create blood clots: if a Kapha type develops a stroke, this will be due to a clot and not to an aneurysm.

Fiery type (Pitta)

The main features of a fiery nature are *heat* and *regularity*. It is a person characterized by irascibility and extroversion who shows an acute element of critical thought. They are critical of themselves and others and their aim is to change them for the better by offering to "organize" things and situations. In fact, if people do not follow their suggestions, they will do things themselves to show that they know better.

The health problems related to this type have to do more with the element of *heat* and *inflammation*. They tend to develop skin problems from simple acne and spots or pimples to eczema and psoriasis. They often complain about problems with gastritis in the form of ulcers or a burning feeling in the stomach.

They often develop ulcerative colitis, inflammatory bowel disease (IBD) and hemorrhoids (piles) while their liver and pancreas may function poorly. They have sensitive capillary veins and be prone to nosebleeds while Pitta women have problems with the menstrual fluids. If they suffer a stroke, it will be a hemorrhagic-type stroke. They also tend to suffer from anaemia and have problems with their vision.

The Ayurverdic types correspond to George Paschalidis' typology in the following way:

Airy type (Vata):	Type **A**
Watery/earthy type (Kapha):	Type **B**
Fiery Type (Pitta):	Type **C**

It is worth noting that the diseases that Ayurveda considers as characteristic for each type match exactly what Paschalidis 'sees'. There are also many similarities in the traits of the characters described.

Rosenman-Friedman

In the 1950s, two American cardiologists, Ray Rosenman and Meyer Friedman, observed that many of their patients with cardiovascular problems had many common behavioral characteristics.

Based on this observation, they developed a theory according to which people are classified into three personality types.

The personality of *Type A* is marked by distinctive characteristics such as ambition, intense competitiveness, impatience, constant alertness and the desire for rapid social rise and recognition.

The personality of *Type B* relates to people that are patient, slack and unhurried, They are often considered apathetic and remote.

The personality of *Type AB* relates to people that show the characteristics of both the aforementioned types (A and B).

The Rosenman-Friedman types correspond to GeorgePaschalidis' typology in the following way:

Rosenman-Friedman	Paschalidis
Type **A**	Type **A**
Type **B**	Type **B**
Type **AB**	Type **C**

In the table that follows, we compare the similarities between the theories developed over time with regard to the human personality and the natural features that form and influence it. As a basis for our comparison we stress the triadic element, although in some historical sources the factors influencing personality appear to be four or even more.

It does appear, however, that the triadic structure is a pivotal element in Creation (God created man in his own image). The human skeletal structure has been fully confirmed through the vision granted to me.

George Paschalidis	Hippocrates - Galen	Ayurveda
A TYPE Man of the "air" Intelligent Indefatigable Spontaneous Forward- looking Humorous Disorganized **DISEASES** Multiple Sclerosis Epilepsy Senility	**SANGUINE** Air Lively Sentimental Unstable Joyous	**AIRY TYPE (VATA)** Perpetual motion Disorganized Fickle Spontaneous Creative Without a schedule Artistic Smart, Quick **DISEASES** Multiple sclerosis Epilepsy Senility
B TYPE Reserved Overanxious, Deliberate Conservative Serves others Feels underprivileged Professions: accountant, secretary, nurse, doctor	**PHLEGMATIC** Water Reticent Sentimental	**WATERY/EARTHY** (KAPHA) Laid-back Slow Prudent Shy Mild
C TYPE Extreme Dwells on old grievances	**CHOLERIC-MELANCHOLIC** Fire, Sad, Apathetic Solitary	**FIERY TYPE (PITTA)** Irascible Egocentric Abrupt Judgmental

Plato	Aristotle	Plutarch
REASONING/ RULERS Synthetic thinking Administrative capacities	**DIALECTIC** Seeks the essence of things	**PRACTICAL** Man of action
SPIRITED/ SOLDIERS Sentimental	**CONSERVATIVE** Slow Prudent	**CONTEMPLATIVE** Man of reason Man of theory
APPETITIVE- WORKERS Produces and offers goods and services Hard-working	**HEDONISTIC- SENSUOUS** Seeks pleasures Pleasant Sweet/amiable	**PLEASURE LOVING** Seeks pleasures Pleasant Sweet/amiable

A new knowledge of old truths

Today there is a *new theoretical appraisal of man.* It is *A NEW KNOWLEDGE,* both in the way it is acquired and the results thereby obtained. We are certain we will transform the lives of all the people in the middle term. This is not a figure of speech. Medical science will soon benefit from this knowledge, making peoples' lives all over the world *easier.*

We have not written this book expecting that it will be accepted or endorsed immediately. What I implore you to do is to follow the thread unfolding in this book, without prejudice and with an open mind. I have written down, for your benefit, all that I have experienced and all that I have lived through. I am disseminating this knowledge in order to help your physical and mental health, and, above all, I an conveying a message that may change your lives.

THE THREE PERSONALITY TYPES ACCORDING TO GEORGE PASCHALIDIS

The role of the vertebrae

I have already mentioned my unique discovery that for the entire human race there are three skeletal structures. This is the idea I intend to clarify in the following pages. I came to these conclusions having 'seen' and grasped the differences there are between people.

What is unique with my typology is that **the differences in the skeletal structures** of people define their classification in **three types**. These types I call **A, B** and **C**.

The differences in our skeletal structure that classify us in one of the three types are located in the cervical area, and more specifically in the cervical vertebrae and the first thoracic vertebrae.

The development of our character and our behavior, as well as the particular sensitivities in matters of mental and physical health all depend on the **cervical section.** The cervical column or spine is divided into five areas or sections. The cervical section comprises seven vertebrae. This section of the vertebral column is extremely important because all the neurons (nerve cells) that link the brain to the body, as well as all the arteries that supply the brain with oxygen, pass through this area and, depending on its structural peculiarities, it influences the function of the entire human body.

Thus, depending on the point of the vertebrae where the variation or differentiation occurs –we are interested particularly in the first four vertebrae and the intervertebral sections (C1-C2, C2-C3, C3-C4) – different pressure is applied to the cervix, which results in the creation of each of the three types. Depending on where the pressure point is located, different sensitivities are created and corresponding physical problems occur. Therefore, different problems will be created in the body depending on the type (A, B, C type).

The three types of skeletal structure

Skeletal structure of type A:

In this case, it is observed that we may have a narrower intervertebral section between the first and the second cervical vertebra (C1- C2). The greater this disorder is, the more the nerve roots are damaged. The more the nerve roots are under stress, the more the pressure on the back of the neck. This leads to a disorder of the jugulars (diastolic blood pressure).

Skeletal structure of type B:

There is a narrower intervertebral section between the second and the third vertebra (C2-C3) resulting in nerve root damage and which exerts pressure on the thyroid gland. Thus gradations (hyperthyroidism, hypothyroidism or bronchial rupture) and affectations appear in the aural nerves and the thymus gland, causing a problem to the central artery of the heart through electric signals resulting in irregular episodes (atrial fibrillation). High blood pressure (systolic) also occurs.

Skeletal structure of type C

Sensitivity is located in the third and fourth cervical

vertebra (C3-C4), where there is a narrower intervertebral section. This results in the friction of the nerve roots that pass through this section. Consequently, pressure is exerted on the pancreatic gland passing through the cervical section. We say that the person with such a skeletal structure functions in a lymphatic way.

I am often asked whether a person may change his type during his lifetime. This is not possible because the type is determined by the skeletal structure of the body and this cannot change.

Depending on the environment, the parents, the surrounding conditions, the personal pursuits and experiences, we may ascertain qualitative variations in each type. However, our extreme reactions (those occurring under pressure) are always given within our type and faithfully follow its parameters. *The desideratum for each type is to create the best possible balance within one's own type.* It is then that the beauty of each one of us will emerge in its full splendor. It is only then that we can be more complete and authentic. We can take control of ourselves and we become freer than ever before. We proceed happily down our own personal path.

There are no good or bad types. *It is the extreme manifestations of each type that creates the problems and the frictions.* Problems expressed with the first type (A) are expressed with irritation, with the second (B) with anxiety and with the third (C) with stubbornness. When these extreme manifestations last too long, the result is to poison the human and ultimately weaken the body.

The way to restore balance varies for each type. *Type A must get rid of the irritation regarding the present, type B must free himself from anxiety about tomorrow and type C from the pain about yesterday.*

But if we manage to avoid or control our extreme reactions, all of us, irrespective of our type, will reconcile ourselves to our type, come to terms with it and enjoy life by becoming calm, patient and tolerant towards others.

Genetic origin of the types

The role of the dominant gene

Although there are three skeletal types, determining the three different temperaments (A for action, B for anxiety and C for order and the absolute), there are six human characters depending on whether one has taken at the moment of his birth the dominant gene from one's father (e.g. if he is A♂* – A type from his father) or the mother (e.g. he is A♀** – A type from mother). I have "seen" that the dominant, superior gene of the new human being that is born is one, and comes from the parent that, during conception, presents the highest defense, i.e. the lowest disorder. In other words, it comes from the parent that during the time of conception was organically in the best condition.

In the cases that we have inherited the dominant gene from our father, which means that the dominant element is the male, it is almost certain that we tend to express ourselves in a more abrupt and agitated manner. Our characteristic behavior becomes more extroverted but less diplomatic. When the dominant gene comes from the mother (that is, if our mother had a lower disorder during the time of our conception thus making the female gene dominant), then we tend to express ourselves in a milder and mellower manner. We tend to explain ourselves through reason

---

* ♂ Stands for male dominant gene
** ♀ Stands for female dominant gene

and not through irritation we are more introverted and tolerant.

If our gene comes from the father, our reaction is spontaneous. If our gene comes from the mother, our reaction is more thought-out. This is due to the fact that men are always in a condition of readiness (for action in the case of type A, for anxiety in the case of type B and for order in the case of type C) and this is expressed through agitation. On the contrary, if our gene comes from the mother, there is laxness in reactions. In this case, all three human types express their feelings mildly, tend to explain themselves politely and claim one's rights through the use of argument.

Male thinking is quick and direct, in contrast to female thinking that analyzes things patiently, but lacks a quick reaction.

In cases where the dominant gene corresponds to the genetic sex (e.g. the male gene and male gender correspond) then the individual is complete.

When a man has received the dominant gene from the father, he "runs" with the speed of thought and his body follows. The man, however, who has received the dominant gene from the mother, is marked by a kind of thinking that puts the brakes on his speed and in the immediacy of his reactions.

When a woman has received the dominant gene from the father, the male gene shows dynamism in thinking. That is, it exhausts the female body and does not permit the woman to enjoy her female nature. The woman has already registered in her genes the purpose of procreation. When she receives the dominant gene from her mother, then she is tormented, as she is trapped between the procreative thinking and a need to explain everything through reason.

My experience with thousands of people firmly confirms the above differentiations between the various types with regard to the genetic origin of the type. The process of passing on the dominant gene is explained in the chapter "Conception and Pregnancy".

The three human types in detail

In the following pages, I will present in detail elements for the recognition of our skeletal structure, the three dominant personalities and the physical sensitivities of each type. Because these sensitivities may emerge in the course of our life, *it is good that people know what they are* in order to better protect their body.

The list of predispositions means exactly what the word suggests. They are *predispositions*. I do not claim that we will definitely get sick. These dispositions are analyzed here in order to both exemplify what the different types are more clearly and to facilitate better prevention. I should stress once more that it is not certain that *the physical sensitivities described will definitely occur.* This depends on the level of disorder one has. If the disorder is high, then *and only then* will they occur and we will suffer the disease.

If the reader recognizes signs or symptoms on themselves or their family in what will follow, it is advisable that they does not make a diagnosis themselves but visit his physician.

TYPE A

Skeletal structure

The sensitivity is located in the first cervical vertebra, the 'Atlas'. Atlas presses the base of the brain. People belonging to type A show a narrower gap between the first and the second intervertebral space (C1-C2) which causes injury to the nerve roots passing through the cervix. Because of this injury, a problem occurs in the thoracic carotid, while at the same time a wider space is created between the seventh cervical vertebra and the first thoracic vertebra, resulting in problems with arthritis.

Personality
Cerebral person
Makes snap decisions
Dynamic and productive
Proud
Sets goals and implements them without waiting for the approval of others
Overcomes obstacles quickly and rejects whatever bothers him
Is self-confident
Is spontaneous
Openly expresses openly their annoyance
Explosive, not in control of what they say or do, but calms down quickly and forgets all about it
Impatient
Low tolerance to pressure
Is a free thinking
Is a leader, a pioneer

Easily makes others follow them

Has "wings" andneeds to be constantly on the move, to "fly"

A person of the "air", does not stop anywhere, moves ahead, often living in their own world

Physical predispositions

Increased cerebral pressure (increased haematosis of the brain)

Sensitive organs: brain, stomach, rectum (the last part of it)

Cirrhosis of the liver (of psychogenetic cause)

Ophthalmologic: myopia, keratoconus (mainly in the right eye)

Predisposition for stroke (haemorrhage, on the right or left temple)

Epileptic seizures

Multiple sclerosis

Displacement of the nasal septum

Alzheimers

Schizophrenia - hallucinations

Angina

Diastolic hypertension

Tachycardia

Pneumonia
Thromboembolism
Gastrointestinal bleeding
Increase of liver enzymes (psychogenetic)
Cutaneous lupus erythematosus
Inflammations of the joints
Polymyalgia
Development of gall stones and kidney stones in the right kidney
High triglycerides (psychogenetic causes)
Hemorrhoids
Constipation
Brain cancer (tumor in the left or right temple area)
Throat cancer
Tongue cancer
Lung cancer
Large intestine cancer
Stomach cancer (interior)
Kidney cancer (left kidney)
Liver cancer (even number of tumors)
Type A is the only one that can develop cancer of the thyroid (cold nodules)

TYPE B

Skeletal structure

The particularity of type B is due to the second cervical vertebra. The second intervertebral space, between the second and the third cervical vertebrae (C2 -C3), appears to be narrower, thus injuring the nerve roots passing through. Similarly, the acoustic nerve and the thyroid are affected. A "step", a shift between the seventh intra-vertebral space and the first thoracic vertebra, also appears, which is responsible for rheumatism and numbness. The first thoracic vertebra also protrudes, thus exerting pressure on the nearby nerve glands.

Personality

Emotional

Patient

Reserved

Has self-control in words and actions

Romantic

Conscientious

Giving person, always retaining something for himself, though

Measured person, calculates excessively every

action, avoids risks, only ventures from a position of safety

Hesitant

Security-oriented

Needs encouragement

Prone to excuses

Quite diplomatic

Speaks quite analytically, always starts with an introduction, to prepare their interlocutor, careful not to upset them, his talk circles around the same point

Born to serve, although impatient he continues to serve the others

He never asks for something, he finds it difficult to take from others so people must insist on it

He often feels wronged and complains

He expects recognition

He cries easily

Man of "water", he tries hard to find the right solution

Always on the move to catch up with everything

Physical predispositions

Type B shows sensitivity in the area of parathyroid glands, he may develop nodules, hyperthyroidism, hypothyroidisms and goiter.

Moto-neuron disease

Parkinson's disease

Dysarthria

Tinnitus

Retrobulbar neuritis

Astigmatism, myopia, macular degeneration, retinal detachment (to a greater degree on the right eye)

Ankylosing spondylitis

Vasculitis

Mitral valve prolapse

Atrial fibrillation

Aneurysm

Thrombophilia

Spastic bronchitis

Spastic colitis

Gastroesophageal reflux

Thalassemia

Psoriasis (in the entire body, mainly the face)

Inguinal hernia

Phlebitis

Rheumatoid arthritis

Degenerative arthritis (knees)

Chondrocalcinosis (accumulation of crystals in the joints)

Burning feet syndrome

Numbness and tingling in the hands

Should Type B people develop cystic pimples during adolescence, there is a possibility that they will be left with scars on the face

High levels of cholesterol and lipids (of genetic etiology)

Calculi or gallstones

Nephrolithiasis (on the right kidney)

Internal hemorrhoids (10cm before the rectum)

Brain tumor (multiple dispersed tumors)

Multiple myeloma

Astrocytoma

Lung cancer (to the one of them)

Colon cancer (9.5 cm from the rectum)

Kidney cancer (to the left one)

Liver cancer (even number of tumors)

Particularly in women: cystic mastitis, resulting in the development of cancer in the right breast, which relapses in the mediastinum and the right lung and is of hormonal etiology.

B type men are the only ones who can develop breast cancer.

Testicular cancer (left testicle)

Melanomas

Rheumatoid lupus erythematosus, with intolerable pain in the bones (due to the sensitivity of B type people to rheumatoid arthritis).

TYPE C

Skeletal structure

Type C's sensitive point is located between the third and fourth cervical vertebrae (C3-C4).

The intervertebral space between the third and fourth cervical vertebrae (C2-C3) is narrower. As a result, the nerve roots which pass through the neck are strained at that particular location. Type C exhibits visible kyphosis from the sixth cervical to the second thoracic vertebra. Such kyphosis causes osteoarthritis and severe skeletal problems.

Personality

A passionate person given to extremes

Idealistic

Ambitious

Competitive

Exhibits leadership qualities

Generous. Gives everything, but when disillusioned wants everything back.

Extreme

Feels a lot of pain (physically and emotionally)

Constantly goes back to old griefs and recycles them

Does not leave problems behind, does not forget them. They carry with them in order to torment themselves.

Very interested in their image

Organized

Demanding

Insecure

Afraid of rejection

Absolute

Insatiable

Always tormented by the question "why". Why don't they understand them? Why wasn't everything done according to their way?

A person of "fire", "scorches" themselves and/or others.

Physical predispositions

Type C is generally the most vulnerable and may exhibit:

Malfunction of the pancreas due to lack of pancreatic enzymes

Blood conditions (anaemia, leukaemia)

Kidney conditions (left): cysts, urine retention, kidney failure (may need dialysis)

Brain hemorrhage (in all parts of the brain except temporal parts)

Meningitis

Mitochondrial encephalopathy (due to the lack of Q10 coenzymes)

Cysts and hernias of the cervical and lumbar regions

Varicocele

Myopia, astigmatism, hyperopia, macular degeneration, glaucoma and diseases of the retina (mainly in the left eye, the condition of which may deteriorate)

Circulatory diseases

Systolic and diastolic hypertension

Couperose

Sudden increase of blood sugar levels (of psychogenic etiology; may require insulin)

Lactose intolerance

Gangrene

Pulmonary edema

Gastroesophageal reflux disease

Mud and sand in the gall bladder, which results in pancreatitis

Increase of LDL cholesterol (of psychogenic etiology)

Allergic asthma

Allergic bronchitis

Allergic shock

Obstructive pulmonary disease

Dermatitis – eczemas

Osteoarthritis

Autoimmune diseases, such as systemic lupus erythematosus, Hashimoto's thyroiditis, extensive vitiligo, scleroderma

Crohn's disease

Lipomas

Osteomas (minor external tumor under the epidermis)

Fibroadenomas (mainly in left breast and lymph nodes)

Lymphomas

Glioblastoma (a type of brain cancer)

Pancreatic cancer, liver cancer (multiple sites), bronchial cancer, lymph node cancer

Colon cancer (in multiple sites)

Kidney cancer (right)

Systemic lupus erythematosus

In C types, the skin, bones and vascular system are

sensitive and are not maintained properly.

Let us reiterate that all of us may develop all diseases. The difference lies in whether the disease we may develop is a disease of our type. In this event, the disease has a tendency to deteriorate.

We note, for example, that psoriasis is a disease pertinent to type B. In a B-type person it may exhibit a particularly serious condition in that it may cover the whole body and face. Psoriasis is an A-type disease, on the other hand, when it develops mildly on the fingers, joints (knees, elbows), genital organs, and may have an appearance similar to dryness of skin. However, it is treated relatively easily and is curable. In a C-type person, psoriasis has an appearance similar to eczema. It may also appear on the face, but it is more easily treatable.

Mentality and behavior of each type

The type of each person is also readily recognizable from the dominant posture of the body, the way he is poised for action and movement.

A. The first type makes decisions quickly, has one leg "always lifted" to make the next step, to proceed to something new, to act. When he suffers a stroke or multiple sclerosis, the aggravation is always on one side of the body, because it is precisely the one leg that is always lifted.

Because he acts spontaneously, both in thinking and in movement, there is an increase in the cerebral blood flow. Because type A has the tendency to move far, to look ahead, perhaps his body "takes revenge" on him or attempts to balance this intense tendency, by developing shortsightedness, thus stopping his need to see far!

B. The second type is hesitant with regard to making decisions and this makes him stand with the one leg suspended for quite some time. One may observe that the body may develop some tremor: this is the main symptom of Parkinson's disease, an affliction of type.

B. Type B has the tendency to withdraw into himself, his internal world (he may suffer from depression) and he ponders and weighs all the goals he wants to attain all the time. He develops astigmatism in the eyes, resulting in blurring the picture, so that he cannot see objects near him. This reflects his "indecisiveness to proceed". The Parkinson tremor does not let him touch objects. He needs someone's support. Finally, with the atrial fibrillation, he needs a pacemaker for support.

C. The third type "does not lift the foot off the ground". He is always stuck, he finds it difficult to detach himself from old situations and from the people that torment him. He stays put to be tormented. When, of course, too much is accumulated, he may "lift both legs and move away". However, he will come back, either in body or in spirit. He may cause great grief to others without his realizing it. Even if he shuns someone, he wants them to come back, if only to take his revenge.

Because he never "lifts his foot", type C is sensitive to afflictions of the lower extremities and he suffers greater pains in the feet. In the eyes, he develops glaucoma; he loses his sight, as he is blinded on a symbolic level of his egotism. He does not, therefore, see things realistically, as they are!

I will continue by citing various *catch phrases* used by representatives of the three types, phrases that reveal their attitude towards life, and I will describe *their reactions to various circumstances.*

Type A proceeds with wings.   *He flies*
Type B proceeds on foot.   *He walks.*
Type C proceeds on his knees.   *He gets stuck.*

If you ask: "How are you?"
Type A will answer: "Just fine!"
Type B will reply: "So and so"
Type C will reply: "I'm struggling". And he will add, stoically, "What else can we do?"

When they come across a ditch, meaning an obstacle:
Type A goes round it easily in seconds.
Type B goes round and round the ditch, contemplating what the best way of surmounting the problem is, thus wasting time.
Type C jumps over the ditch, only to land in the next one, where he remains stuck. He dwells on problems.

When they feel under pressure:
Type A opens the door and leaves.

Type B always shuts himself up in a room (or within himself) in order to "put things in order."

Type C wants to make a change, but does not know what, so he just rearranges the furniture and everything.

Type A is always in a state of alert or relaxation.

Type B is always in a defensive position.

Type C is always on guard.

When things get difficult, or do not add up:

Type A shows panic.

Type B shows anxiety.

Type C shows sadness.

Type A retains all that are to his benefit.

Type B always finds something to keep him busy and is always anxious.

Type C always finds a problem to hang onto in order to punish himself.

The usual reactions of the three types recall their physical sensitivities or their subconscious fears. Thus, they say:

Type A: "I am leaving; leave me alone!" or "You

drive me crazy. I will have a stroke because of you!" or "I'm tired of you! You get on my nerves!"

Type B: "I am fed up with you. I am about to explode!" (because his disposition is characterized by a swelling of the liver and the spleen)

Type C: "You've driven me up the wall" or as the Greeks would say: "You have eaten me alive!", because his disposition is to "eat himself" with the self-immunization he develops when his disorder is increased.

When they feel that nobody understands them:

Type A people leave, so that they will make others understand them.

Type B waits until he is understood.

Type C is exasperated that he is not understood.

Type A lives in the present, every moment of it.

Type B feels anxious about tomorrow, and does not live today.

Type C sticks in the past and misses out on today.

Type A likes going downhill because it is easier

B type likes the even plane because he can go round and round

Type C prefers going uphill to go out of breath and torment himself
Type A mostly feels satisfaction
Type B feels more the sentiment
Type C mostly experiences passion

Type A is a man of action
Type B is a man of anxiety
Type C is a man of "order"

When things get hard on them:
Type A feels pressure on his chest
Type B feels a "tightness' in his chest
Type C feels a lump in his throat, a punch to the stomach and, sometimes, a stubbing to his back, if things get really bad.

Type A cannot be stuck to any particular problem. He attempts to solve it. If he does, he leaves it alone. If the problem cannot be solved, he leaves it behind and moves on.

Type B is an anxious person and insists on solving the problem. He is always in expectation of the solution.

Type C tries hard to solve the problem and insists on conquering it.

After a disagreement:

Type A says "Let's sort it out now and get it over it."

Type B keeps it within himself for a long time and bursts out some time in the future. In this way, the problem is never sorted out.

Type C must definitely sort it out or else he cannot find peace. He will be tormented until he finds a solution.

Some examples from everyday life:

If you offend them on the meal they have prepared for you:

Type A will throw the lid of the saucepan at you and shout "Come and do it yourself!"

Type B will start sobbing over the saucepan, but will continue stirring the food because he couldn't bear see it go to waste.

Type C will not say anything to you, but if you insist, he will throw the entire content of the kitchen cupboards on your head.

If you step on them:

Type A either will punch you or will tell you "leave me alone" and go away.

Type B will first look around to see how many have witnessed his humiliation and see if there is any way to react.

Type C will react by leaving. As he does, he will think he did not say what he should have and come back to sort things out.

In an argument:

Type A will throw whatever he finds in front of him without consideration of how valuable it may be (for example, an expensive glass).

Type B will think about it and instead of throwing a valuable item, he will throw away something that he does not need (for example, the straw in the glass).

Type C will show some patience, but in the end he will throw the entire table.

If they are invited to a wedding and a funeral on the same day:

Type A will cry in the funeral in the morning and dance in the wedding on the same evening.

Type B will not go nowhere because he is afraid that he will be commented negatively.

Type C will only go to the funeral, since he will think: "I have no place at a wedding."

Type A often speaks with the eyes, he is an immediate type.

Type B speaks a lot through the mouth.

Type C speaks through his entire being (moving hands and legs)

When it is raining:

Type A does not care, he is indifferent, come rain or shine.

Type B feels anxious about it, and starts counting the raindrops.

Type C goes and sits in the rain to get wet.

If a bridge is to collapse:

Type A will pass safely under it and the bridge will collapse two hours later.

Type B will still be at home preparing.

Type C will be on the bridge or under it when it falls.

When they speak:

Type A moves only the one arm, as if he is broadcasting

Type B moves only the one finger, as if he is a teacher

Type C moves both his arms and his legs simultaneously.

When they offer something:

Type A gives and goes.

Type B gives, looks in your eyes and asks whether you are happy with it.

Type C gives and doesn't ask anything. If you say you do not like it he is going to hit you on the head with it.

Type A lives for himself and gives to others too.

Type B lives for the others, gets anxious, and does not give either to himself or toe others.

Type C lives through the others (so that he puts their lives in order) and ends up tormenting both himself and the others.

If Type A reaches the point of suicide, first attempts suicide and then asks himself "have I committed suicide?"

If Type B comes to the point of contemplating suicide, he is so timid about it that he keeps finding one excuse after the other for not doing it, and gives himself another chance, thinking that he is too indispensable to the others and does not want to upset them so much by killing himself.

Type C organizes everything to perfection. He

leaves a suicide note in which he blames everyone else so that they feel guilty. He needs to clarify this. He prepares a year for this. If he finally does commit suicide, he does it in an impeccable manner. He stages his suicide.

In general:

Type A jettisons all problems, so that he is not bothered by them.

Type B presents fluctuations, all day. He remembers sometimes the pleasant things and sometimes the unpleasant ones.

Type C remembers only the unpleasant things, in order to torment himself.

The relation to dependencies, alcohol, smoking, substances, gambling:

Type A if ever is to get into the temptation, if he decides to quit, he frees himself relatively easily.

Type B is difficult to quit, if he develops a dependency.

Type C is instant. He may start drinking, then quit, go through rehabilitation, and then start all over again.

If a friend has a problem:

Type A encourages him. He says: "It is nothing at all", and tries to make him laugh.

Type B looks at him in the eyes all anxious and thus burdens him with his own anxiety as well!

Type C narrates his own difficulties he has been through, and at the end they cry together!

When they find themselves at an impasse – when the ship is sinking:

Type A dares, and also tends do all he can help.

Type B does not dare to do a thing, is panicked and is anxious that the ship is sinking.

Type C, as soon as he realizes that the ship is sinking, gets under the ship saying "where can it go, I will save it!"

The professions they choose, that 'give them life' are:

Type A will choose to be self-employed.

Type B will be a nurse, doctor, teacher or secretary.

Type C is not prone to choosing a difficult or demanding profession. Many artists belong to type C. Moreover, it is the type of many hobbies.

If they see a bunch of grapes hanging from the vine, and they set their eyes to have some, this is how they will go about it:

Type A stretches to reach them, and if he can't make it will leave saying "they are not ripe."

Type B looks around, circumspect lest people comment negatively on him, and does not even try.

Type C, when he realizes that he cannot reach them, immediately thinks that he must have them. This and only this is what he wants. He fetches ladders, organizes a whole expedition to grab the bunch of grapes. He falls from the ladder, keeps trying for a month to reach his goal, the grapes go off... He finally manages to eat them nevertheless and comments that they are very sweet.

The three types *as parents*:

Type A encourages his child to leave home, to spread his wings and go. Others think of him as insensitive.

Type B always points out to his child the dangers (to be careful not to 'fall'), resulting in the child never leaving in order not to fail, not to 'fall'. Moreover, very diplomatically he fills the child with guilt so that the latter does not desert him.

Type C initially admonishes the child to leave, but then, due to his feelings of insecurity pulls the child towards him or goes by him.

To the question "Are you an egotist?" they respond:

Type A replies that he is a bit.

Type B answers "everyone is a bit, why not me?"

Type C responds: "Not in the least!"

In their utterances:

Type A in one word says it all.

Type B starts with a long prologue, trying to explain and not displease you, but finally ends up trying your patience.

Type C first recasts the past and then is absolute in what he says.

Let us now see how they three types converse in the world. If, for example they enter a room with many people in it.

Type A will enter confidently; he may greet the others but will not pay much attention to their reactions.

Type B will enter politely and modestly, trying not to attract attention.

Type C, much to the contrary, will fight a lot with himself before entering and then will try to become the focus of attention, he needs this alot.

Type A dresses for himself and only for himself. Sometimes elegantly sometimes casually, depending on how he feels at the time.

Type B dresses very conservatively, trying not to draw much attention, but at the end he does precisely the opposite. His dress code is very careful. Women tend to wear two and three blouses at a time.

Type C dresses in order to attract attention. A man more easily would wear an earring or a flashy leather jacket. A type C woman easily would combine red shoes with a red handbag, net socks, rings on her toes and perhaps on all fingers, the index and the thumb. If she happens to be a feminine type C she would also wear flashy and daring jewelry like a cross pendant 15 cm long and she may torment her body with body piercing like earrings on the nose, the eyebrow, the nipples or the navel.

The same stressful event affects:

Type A by 30%

Type B by 50%

Type C by 100%

Finally, the distribution of the three types in the entire earth population is:

Type A percentage reaches 15%.

Type B percentage is 25%.

Type C percentage reaches 60%.

The male and the female dominant gene

I continue with some examples and observations on the ways the male dominant gene manifests itself (♂ from the father) and the female dominant gene (♀ from the mother) when it dominates in one of the three types:

A. THE FIRST TYPE

The A♂man is dynamic, with leadership qualities and tendencies. He expresses himself verbally very clearly, he says it all in one word, but does not have the time to sit and explain it. He is both a "lion" and a "baby", depending on how you approach him. If you annoy him he will come out as a lion, if you hug him, the baby appears.

He is the unquestionable leader. If pressed, he retorts "leave me alone" and leaves. He returns, however, a bit later, as if nothing happened. And indeed, nothing happened for him.

For example, once an A♂ man paid me a visit, and when I asked him "what is it that you want", he replied, "nothing", he just came to see.

The typeA♀ man shows dynamism, leadership qualities and abilities, yet he comports himself with a milder, more amiable style. He is a lion in the body with a feminine mind that makes him feel the need to explain the reason behind everything he does. He is lion tied with chains. Explosively introvert, he erupts inwardly. He may leave if pressed, yes, but he feels like returning to explain why.

The A♂ woman is a person of action. That is, she runs for everyone and everything and does not have time for herself. All she can offer to herself is something ready-made like a toast or sandwich.

An A♂ woman has inherited her mother's health problems but she also has problems with her leg and limps. As soon as I finished with her mother I offered to check her too.

"There is nothing wrong with me. I am OK!" she insisted.

Despite her protestations that she had no problem at all, I helped her and she left with no limp at all, walking normally.

The A♀woman, on the other hand
leadership qualities with flexibility, femin
and nervousness, and she tends to react by
to crying. She does possess the patience to a
goals, but the nervousness of her type does no. .er her
enjoy them. Emotionally she is an introvert person,
and she has a talent for talk. The A♀ woman has flair
and she accustoms herself to the surrounding easily,
in seconds, but she is easily carried away and tries to
assume a leadership role.

B. TYPE B

In type B, the differences between male and female
are minuscule, because it is a type in itself and is
generally introvert and dative, giving, because it
functions more motherly. Men and women who
belong to B type and have inherited the dominant
gene from their father (♂) externalize their anxiety
through movement and in general act easier and
more intensely than a Bman or woman from the
mother. In contrast, B types from their mother keep
everything in themselves and externalize their anxiety
later, using much talk and excuses.

For example, I remember a lady B(♂) that had
come with her husband who had a health problem.
After examining her husband I asked her whether

she needed some help too.

"I didn't come for me but for my husband", she retorted.

"But you also have a health problem", I explained to her.

"It doesn't matter. I came for my husband", she insisted.

I reiterated for a third time.

"Should I also check you"?

"No, no, just my husband!"

Despite all this, I finally did help her.

I stress that type B never asks for help, and never easily accepts help, although he does feel the need for it deep inside him. One has to insist.

Once I asked a type B♀ lady.

"Why have you come?"

"I do not know. Take a guess!" she replied.

C. THE THIRD TYPE

Type C, on the contrary, although presenting the same physical sensitivities, also manifests a great differentiation with regards to behavior.

If a man who is type C from the father (C♂) has the same leadership characteristics as man who is type A from the father (A♂), he will get stuck when confronted with a problem. He cannot surmount it, as type A would. As a result, he is tormented with himself.

If a man who is type C from the mother (C♀) appears to be amiable and mild, he remains stubborn, without yet saying what he thinks ought to be done. But he does it.

A woman who is type C from the father (C♂) differs markedly from her female nature. She runs from problem to problem. Her thoughts are constantly in motion and action, setting difficult tasks, without yet enjoying anything.

These women function like 'men'. Their souls run at a speed of a thousand miles an hour whilst their body is set for a speed of fifty, resulting in abusing their bodies. A type C♂ woman is so fast at everything that she can only arrange things without ever having the time to enjoy anything. Something like: "We ate, we cleaned up after us, we polished everything behind and we left". She is absolute, strict with herself and she is tormented.

I remember a C♂ lady who once paid me a visit for some problems with her arms. Stressed out, she pointed out to me:

For years now I haven't been able to lift a thing. I have gone round to the best doctors, to the professors, I have paid a fortune, but with no result, I haven't seen any improvement.

I "see" that her problem originates from the cervix and I tell her so.

"No, I can't believe this is the cause", she objects.

"So, why did you come to me, if you have no intention of listening to me", I am baffled.

"Because I have had enough with living like this, with my arms dangling down..."

I help her urging her to lift her left arm, and she does so, without realizing she has lifted an arm. She admits that the pain is less, but she insists the pain is still there. I try again, and she is lifting her arm high, declaring flatly that there is no pain at all. But she was still annoyed.

"Do you wish to come next month, to check the other arm too?" I asked her, smiling.

"No", she stops me abruptly, "I want it checked now!"

I go on offering her some more help, and I ask her to raise the right arm. She does so, and although everyone around is flabbergasted how she managed do this, she is smiling, nonplussed, as if nothing big happened.

A type C♀ woman is very direct in her talk, but she

is marked by a lack of diplomacy, and in her external appearance she wants to be extreme, either too manly or too feminine.

On the other hand, though, a type C♀ woman from the mother, enjoys the pain, the difficulties, the tears, and above all her feminine nature. These women share many features with type B. They are the sweetest women, they keep caressing themselves and the others, and they like hugging. Their problem is that they torment themselves because they think others torment them and this occurs because they are very doting, giving.

To make the character of type C♀ women more apparent, I compare them with a mat.

"Everyone steps on you and all exploit you", I tease type C♀ women.

And they retort, somewhat aggressively, somewhat hurt, or even teasingly too: "Why, haven't people truly stepped on me. Haven't they exploited me?"

The three types and diseases

With the first and second type, when diseases occur, they usually affect the right side, and the disease in these cases may take the wrong turn and deteriorate.

With the third type, it is the left side that suffers.

In the case of a stroke:

With type A the brain damage is non-reversible and proves detrimental to the patient's life.

Type B manifests some small incidents of thrombosis that cause brief lapses in thought affecting speech, memory gaps and mobility problems (Parkinson). He may suffer up to fifteen thrombosis episodes without his mobility being severely affected.

Type C may suffer many hemorrhagic episodes that nevertheless could prove reversible even after the occurrence of paralysis or spasticity.

With types A and B the right shoulder slightly bends a bit downwards, while with type C it is the left shoulder that bends somewhat.

An easy exercise in order to avoid burdening the spinal column is to place our shoulder bag on the shoulder that bends downward in order to force it to lift higher. In other words, types A and B should place the carrier bag to the right shoulder whilst type C on the left.

Also, when scoliosis occurs to the spinal column, with types C the arc appears to go to the right, resulting with a 'pull' that causes diastasis of the left kidney and fall of the right. The result is retention of urine, cyst and urinary tract infections. On the contrary, types B manifest the arc of the scoliosis towards the left side, the hip shows a tilt to the back and diastasis occurs on the right kidney, with a possible fall of the left one. Type A does not usually show such problems, yet he may present diastasis to the right kidney.

Stomach problems:
Type A suffers from gastric heartburn.
Type B suffers from acid fluids.
Type C feels pain.

When they rise suddenly:
Type A feels dizzy and sees 'stars'.
Type B feels his head spinning.
Type C tilts his head backwards.
When the disturbance protracts:
Type A may expel the calcium oxalate from his skin (dry skin) and his liver, resulting to liver deficiency.

Type B deposits it on the joints causing degenerative alterations (Ankylosis spondylitis, Chondropatheia etc.).

Type C deposits it in the blood, resulting in the blockage of the arteries (arteriosclerosis) and coronary arteriosclerosis.

If type A shows discoid lupus erythematous, the symptoms would affect the skin (jaundice).

With types B the symptoms of the discoid lupus erythematous affect the bones.

Types C show discoid lupus erythematous mainly in the organs.

With the passage of the years:

Type A may suffer from Alzheimer's disease.

Type B may suffer from temporary lapses due to thrombosis.

Type C may present the oncoming of senility due to the deterioration of his brain arteries and cells.

Type A shows schizophrenia and hallucinations.

Type B, because he is always absorbed in his own views, when withdrawing into himself suffers from depression.

Type C suffers from bipolar depression.

Type A presents intense headaches.

Type B suffers from migraines due to the osseous labyrinth

Type C suffers from vertigo due to kyphosis.

Type A often suffers from pneumonia.

Type B suffers from bronchitis.

Type C suffers from allergic bronchitis and allergic asthma.

Type A feels heartburn in the esophagus.

Type B feels sourness in the esophagus.

Type C feels pains in the esophagus.

Type A suffers from constipation.

Type B suffers from spastic colitis (irritable bowel syndrome).

Type C suffers from constipation and spastic colitis.

Type A must be aware of and check his liver enzymes.

Type B must check often his lipids and his cholesterol levels (increase of the levels due to genetic etiology)

Type C should rein in his sugar and cholesterol levels (increases due to psychogenetic causes).

Type A presents fluctuations of his iron levels.

Type B shows lack of vitamins D and B12.

Type C shows deficiency of vitamin C.

Type A is the only type that may become extraordinarily obese (reach up to 300 kilos).

Type B, when gaining weight, tends to become 'round' and have a protruding belly.

Type C may develop anorexia nervosa or bulimia.

Men, usually after certain age, start losing their hair:

Type A loses hair at the temples and then to the entire scalp. He may develop a local alopecia areata, but this condition is reversible.

Type B loses hair gradually on the top of his head.

Type C loses hair in the front and back on the top. He is the only one that can develop alopecia that can affect the entire scalp.

In regards to hair loss in women, only those of type B lose a noticeable amount of hair on the top of the head.

Women of type C have feeble hair, often blonde, show frizzy hair and loss of hair easier.

Women of type A usually have healthy hair.

The function of the heart in the three types

Type A: The right artery of the heart shows greater speed. The greater the pressure exerted to the brain the feebler the electromagnetic signal sent from the brain to the heart. At some gap, there is confusion resulting in flutter, linked to strokes in the temple area.

Type B: The central artery of the heart shows greater velocity. Problems appear with the small pressure (diastolic). Problems appear with the higher pressure (systolic). The density of the electromagnetic impulses sent from the brain to the heart shows fluctuations, sometime higher some time lower, resulting in arterial fibrillation (ectopic premature verbicular beat).

Type C: More intense emission of the electromagnetic impulse affects both arteries, resulting in pains to the chest and problems in the blood supply the left heart ventricle.

Multiple sclerosis
This disease does not affect a large percentage of the population and the variety of the ways it affects every type of man is significant. There isn't a single type of multiple sclerosis. The disease presents different symptoms in each patient. The symptoms of each person may also show variations from time to time. These characteristics preclude a general description of the disease and an ensuing precise prognosis of its development.

Multiple sclerosis is a self-immunization disease as it is the immune system of the body itself that attacks and destroys the myelin that is the insulation sheath of the nerve fibers.

As myelin acts as insulation for the nerve fiber it protects the quality and intensity of the electrical impulses passing through the nerve fiber. When the insulation sheath is destroyed the electrical impulse is short-circuited or interrupted. The destruction of the insulation of the nerve fibers is caused by local inflammation that, when healed, creates lesions or scleroses to which the disease owes its name. Another name for the disease is diffused encephalomyelitis.

The symptoms vary depending on the spots where the lesions occur, and may include:

Excessive mental and physical fatigue.
Depression.
Mobility problems.
Spasticity.
Vertigo.
Problems with movement coordination.
Disturbances with vision.

When the disease results in disability fast and does not show periods of subdued symptoms or recovery,.

then it is characterized as primary progressive.

Medical science is still trying to ascertain the causes of the disease. It is thought that the main cause is some dysfunction of the immune system (autoimmunization). It is also investigated whether multiple sclerosis may be caused by some serious nervous breakdown or physical injury that may affect directly the immune system.

All diseases, including Multiple Sclerosis, are due to a 'hormonal disorder' factor, that causes some dysfunction in the body, thus weakening its defenses, and their occurrence varies in accordance to the skeletal type. In this sense, MS is exclusively a disease of the immune system.

MS affects mainly type A people and occurs when the levels of disorder are very high, ranging from 56-59 in the scale from 1 to 100. In type A, paralysis occurs vertically on the right side usually and when the disease progresses, to the left side. The patient is constrained to the wheelchair, and may even die. Due to his skeletal structure, type A patients develop areas of outbreak of the disease between the C1 0 C2 vertebrae. However, even persons of types B and C may show demyelination; yet, in many cases medical science finds it difficult to identify the disease because it manifests itself in different ways. 'When medical science does identify the disease it calls it an 'atypical case of Multiple Sclerosis'.

In type B persons, demyelination causes tremor in the legs and instability (it has been pointed out, after all, that Parkinson's disease, a disease sharing many symptoms with MS which is a type B disease, yet MS symptoms come and go). Due to their skeletal structure, type B patients have points of outbreak of the disease between vertebrae C2 – C3.

With type C patients demyelination may cause even paralysis, only of the lower extremities, however, and numbness of the upper extremities. However, after the lapse of five to six years, and if the disturbance is alleviated, type C patients may recover fully and regain their walking. The skeletal structure of type C creates points of outbreak of the disease between vertebrae C3-C4.

One of the most significant variations in the development of the disease Multiple Sclerosis relates to how fast it develops, as with type A patients the development is very rapid, while patients of the other two types, type B and type C it may not show any deterioration even after 20 years.

A second important difference has to do with the fact that with type A patients, the deterioration of the disease is hardly reversible, even after strong chemotherapy.

The examinations of MS patients currently available in Greece would confirm on first instance the typology sketched, and one may easily, using just this process to confirm the typology I propose. In Greece today, there are 8000 victims of MS.

A quick view of the three types

A. THE FIRST TYPE

We already said that he has wings to fly. Usually he runs at a thousand miles per hour. However, if he steps on the breaks suddenly or if his wings are clipped, he may suffer damage.

Type A needs to have the doors open, to glance at the horizon. If he ceases to express himself, to be extroverted, to react, he suffers panic attacks. Tranquilizers and antidepressants with him are quite ill-advised because they clip his wings. Psychotropic drugs are only then advised if he develops a mental disorder.

Type A, and mainly type A from the father, looks the others straight to the eyes. He also talks through the eyes. Type A may say just a word the whole day, but

...he really starts to talk, then he finds it difficult to stop... he gets lost in his own world. Because his voice is coarse, he may develop problems to his vocal chords or even polyps. If, for some reason, he wants to say it all but does not, he suffers from constipation.

Children of type A are independent and 'teasers'.

Type A persons' "medicine" is to praise them, not to antagonize them, not to reject them, not to moan to them. If we smile to them, they would give us everything. Gullibility is their main shortcoming. But if we approach them in a hostile manner, it is as if we tease a lion.

Type A is a proud person, but he may entrap himself in his pride and destroy himself.

B. THE SECOND TYPE

He is a giving person. He is dative and sportsmanlike. Both men and women of this type correspondingly show paternal and maternal instincts. Type B people have come to this life in order to give they only find pleasure and fulfillment in the joy of others. If this is not enough, they appear to carry an antenna on their head, which is noticeable to others who run to unload their burden to them. As Mother Theresa as type B is, it is certain that it is he who will nurse all his relatives in their old age.

He is not so vulnerable to diseases, because he is very aware of them and takes care of himself. After all, as he says, "someone must be in good health in order to take care of others". Often, not only does he give, but also looks the recipient in the eyes to check if he is satisfied. Yet, he also keeps something for himself. He is patient, he is not risky, and he is always in motion in order to catch up with everything. He is a man of excuses, of dialogue.

What is really dangerous for type B is his anxiety that tends to get out of control. At this point it becomes dangerous for his health.

He is the type of person that may return twice or more times to his house to check whether he has locked the door or switched all the lights. He calms down only when he realizes that he has transmitted his anxiety to the others, and then he keeps telling them "do not worry, everything will be just fine!"

Types B may live a long time with the memory of a relationship and often they love in the platonic way.

When, whilst he wants to say something he does not, he suffers from spastic colitis.

Type B moves like the underground: to and fro, to and fro. When one is all right, he is trying to annoy him, but as soon he manages just that, he shrinks back, only to start again as soon as he sees you are smiling again.

Type B always wears a mask, hides behind a smile so that the others do not perceive his anxiety, his real sentiments. He needs a leader by his side, to look up to him and feel proud.

Type B children are spoiled darlings, like kitten.

C. THIRD TYPE

He is the man of passion and extremes. They are usually attractive persons, because they are interested in many things and they are occupied with a vast gamut of activities. Well-informed and multifaceted as they are, they easily charm those around them. They give everything and they demand everything in return. They aim at becoming indispensable to the others. However, they have much sensitivity, physical as well as psychological.

First: They are, deep down, insecure and fearful of rejection, either real or imagined, and interpret others' attitudes as lack of interest. Therefore, they keep trying, keep trying...

Second: They do not free themselves easily from problems in the past. They remember all the pains they suffered since children, regurgitate them, attract problems all the time, and they ache, they ache, they ache...

Third: They do not find it easy to back down, and when proven 'wrong' their ego may drive them to become very upset, whereupon they lash out. And they accuse, they accuse, they accuse...

Fourth: They are unsatisfiable. As soon as they conquer something, they are seduced by something else that they find superior and more valuable than the other, which they abandon before they have time to enjoy it. And they struggle, they struggle, they struggle...

Fifth: As they are extreme types, they give everything but then they demand it back, thereby they give nothing, and only take. Type C persons must learn to only give half and keep the other half for themselves, so that they have something left to give again. Also, they must learn to allow the others room to give as well; otherwise they amass in themselves anger, tormenting both their body and the others, when they become vindictive.

Type C responds with eagerness to uphill challenges. When confronted with a hill, he sets himself the task of conquering it. Half way up the climb, and when he has already paved the way for others to follow, ready at last to reap himself the benefits - enjoying the view, in this case – he glances another top across and he sets to once more struggle uphill to conquer it, once again paving the way to the next ones. He loves to torment himself permanently. He is the one that, when confronted with a problem, he thinks it was created for him and only him, and sets himself out to surmount it.

Type C torments himself because he wants everything in order (his order, he wants everyone to be in order). And because the others do not set things in order, he takes it upon himself to sort it out, on behalf and for the benefit of everyone else. He is the type, let's say, that he may rearrange the place of the furniture in his house time and time again, until he is satisfied. Because his soul is in pain, he wants his body to suffer too.

As children, persons of type C crave for a hug.

Type C gives all his soul; he gives everything and then starts to give bits of his body too. He often participates to causes and organizations with goals that are very hard to attain (he does, after all have the tendency to tilt his head to the left), so that he never has the satisfaction of success, never to have pleasure.

A type C lady from the father, when she heard that type C is an egotist and opinionated, replied in shock:

"But I am not an egotist!'

"Maybe, but it cannot be that we do whatever you want!", I put it to her.

"But if it is right?" she contested.

Then she asked:

"My husband, what type is he?"

"Type C from the mother".

"Well, didn't we have a good relationship?"

Upon which I asked her:

"Where is your husband?"

"He is dead..."

It was with a smile that I declared:

"Well, he had such a lovely time, that he died...the poor chap."

HOW TO BEHAVE TOWARDS OUR LOVED ONES ACCORDING TO THEIR TYPE

In this chapter some specific instructions are put forward regarding the way in which we could behave towards our family and friends, the people we love and they love us, we influence and they influence us.

Perhaps, at first sight, it seems to us that in order to apply these instructions we must show some compromise regarding some annoying behavior on the part of our loved ones so that we have the necessary moderation to treat them according to the special characteristics of their types.

However, if we take under consideration that the extreme (and thus annoying) behaviors of each type take place only when the person is under pressure, then, since we are more relaxed, we could manage the situation cleverly and calm the person.

It is essential, above all, to devote time to fully understand the characteristics of our type, to get to know our own weak points, to become aware of our particularities, to accept them, and finally to love ourselves from the beginning, having knowledge of our nature.

It is very important to keep always in mind that the goal is not to change the other person but to make it easy for him to overcome the obstacles of his type.

A. First type

Type A needs to be praised, not to be opposed, rejected or sniveled about. We know that if we smile at him he becomes very generous.

We saw that he does not wish to speak much, so unless we intend to irritate him, we must respect that.

As he is impatient, we must be punctual in our appointments with him.

Knowing that sometimes he likes to live in his own world, let us help him by giving the chance to withdraw and isolate himself.

We must also respect the fact that he does not like to give explanations and analyze things.

We must avoid hurting his or her pride because if we do he or she becomes very annoyed.

Type A woman has very sensitive nerves. So, let us not irritate her.

It is advised that a type A woman is encouraged to enjoy her successes and devote time to relax and occupy herself with things she likes.

Both type A man and woman are introverted and need to be encouraged to express their feelings.

In two words, with regard to type A man or woman,

We must not irritate them.

We must not speak too much.

We must facilitate their action.

B. Second type

Because type B is sentimental, he needs help when he feels bad. He needs someone to explain to him what he wants in great detail. Then he understands the situation better, gathers strength and gets rid of his anxiety.

He is restrained regarding both acting and speaking and needs encouragement in order to express himself and act.

It is advisable with respect to a type B man or woman:

To advise them to go sometimes on the loose

To encourage them to take risks and make decisions for their lives.

Not to ask them always to justify their actions.

To urge them to tear themselves away from the details.

To show them, even for their small successes, the

recognition that they so much need.

Type B, regardless of gender is born to serve. They may resent some situations but they continue to serve and look after others.

We must always help them to express their needs, because he finds it difficult to take. At the same time they must be taught to contest calmly and resolutely what they consider to be their own.

It important for us not to enhance with our acts or words the feeling of injustice that they nurture for themselves, but to urge them not to complain, but to start enjoying the things that give them pleasure, avoiding to depend his joy on the others.

Finally, type B is sad and needs discreet intervention on our part in order to seek help and avoid depression.

C.Third type

The two basic problems of type C are a permanent insecurity and fear of rejection. Having this in mind, we strengthen their feeling of security and do not scold them.

We must not come into a verbal confrontation with them.

It is good to help them get away from old pains and

problems that they themselves recycle.

Because they are people of extremes we must take care not to push them in this direction.

We must urge them not to involve themselves with unsolvable problems because they become impassioned and suffer.

Especially for women type C from their father (C♂) we must create the proper conditions and give them the chance to enoy their work and relax by devoting time to themselves.

Because the woman who are type C from the father (C♂) is very strict with herself, we must persuade her mildly to relax her self criticism.

We must urge them to show restraint with the generosity of their type and not to exaggerate.
They need help in order to control their fiery temperament.

When we observe that they are attracted and stick to weak persons, it would be good, always calmly, to make sure that they become aware of the specific characteristic of their type and rid themselves of soul destroying relationships.

It is important to help C types to understand that they must give room to others so that they can offer them concern and care.

RELATIONSHIP, PARTNERSHIP
AND FRIENDSHIP

I will now state a few facts in regards to the relationships and particularities that ensue from the types making up a couple.

Two A types make up a harmonious couple. As they are both 'leadership' types but each live in their own world. They are both very active and they are away from home for most of the day. It is a relationship that is intense but at the same time harmonious.

The difficulties start when they have children, and someone must assume the ensuing responsibilities. They begin to feel that the house has become a prison, and the problems start to flow from this. A development frequent in these cases is one of the two develops a stroke or has to be subjected to treatment with psychotropic medicines, and may even die prematurely, because the relationship of the two under the same roof is very intense. When, however, they get to know their type and their reactions, and then they may build a very good relationship, a fact, after all, that holds true to all types.

Type A is a free character, but cannot live alone, he needs his pair. Thus, he gets into a yoke, and "sells" his freedom, but retains his autonomy and freedom of movement.

Often, women who are type A from the father do not get married and live alone. But even if they do get married, they leave very easily. They want the man to be very strong, to take pride in himself, but at the same time, crave for their freedom.

Women who encounter this as the greatest problems in their relationships, are type A from the father, and also type C from the father. This is due to the fact that both types do not easily backtrack; type A because of their nerves and pride, whilst type C because of their stubbornness.

Type B women posing, as they do, no demands in marriage, agree with everything. Thus, given that a type B women is always happy with the happiness of others, makes for an ideal pair for all types. If one asks them how they fare with their marriage, they would answer:

"Never mind, very well. You see, they are men, one must tend to them."

Type B men are more of a symbiotic type, even if they complain a lot, than a woman of type B is. However, marriage is for these men a refuge.

Women who are type C from the father want their men theirs exclusively, and then they give everything. They tend to choose problematic persons. They "rebuild" the others, they adorn them, tidy them up, and these, in return, tend to abandon them without a 'thank you'. But she likes this rebuilding task, and repeats it time and again.

A certain lady, who had been through two marriages (and one relationship with a man of type C) ended up repeating that "there is no man that would honor his trousers."

That time she was in search for this type of man. Her problem was, however, that since she herself felt like a 'man' trapped in a female body, that is, she had a 'male' thinking' running at a speed of a thousand miles an hour whilst her body could stand a speed of no more than fifty, she did not feel either as a man nor as a woman. Thus, she was seeking a man with mixed qualities that would match hers; that is to say, a man that would be dynamic and austere and at the same time mild and gentle.

Yet, this type of man she had in mind does not exist. Therefore, she could not find him.

Type C persons do not easily leave or distance themselves from their relationships. They "stick" very easily to situations of pain, because they wish to be of help.

As my wish is to make all these that I experience 'seeing' people, understood by you, reader, I shall go through the example of a woman that is a characteristic example of such a case.

I recall the case of a lady (Mrs. X) who was type C had come with her husband, who was also type C. Both shared the same serious health problem (both suffered from cancer). I try to "observe" when this problem was created. I find out that the lady had the problem for seven years and the husband for six. Their relationship, including their marriage, had been for four years. Therefore, they got to know each other when they already had their health problem.

"Where did you meet?" I asked.

"Holy Friday, during the Epitaphion procession", was the answer!

Another topic that arises in cohabitation or marriage relates to the management of finances.

If type A has 1000 euros, he will spend 3000 but somehow they will come back to him.

Should type B have 1000 euros, he will spend only 100 but he will not enjoy even this. Things do not come to him easily.

Type C is only interested in being in control of his finances and spends as he likes. He desires to be in control.

If in a relationship, both partners have the same dominant gene, e.g. the male from the father, then none of the two backs down and there is tension in the relationship, because, in this case, both are marked by the rebellious tendency that characterizes the male gene and they cannot put up with problems. Therefore, both erupt and usually leave. Conciliation only comes about when the one of the two backs down, a difficult thing for sure.

When both partners in a relationship have a dominant female gene (from the mother), they consume themselves in a futile dialogue and cannot get rid of the problem by solving it in the dialogue. They are tormented by the thought that a solution be found definitely, because in the mother's gene a birth is inscribed, that begets thinking, the need for justification.

The ideal is for man to have the dominant gene from his father (male) and the woman to have taken it from the mother (female). A balance is obtained then, when the man is for the word – the command – and the woman for thinking – the enforcement of the command.

Marriage is a partnership, and this holds true until obligations arise. In the beginning, when we are in love, we both take because the person in love dares to take! Then, however, comes thinking, and thinking goes on to become a fixation, and both expect to take from the other without giving, with the result that each from his perspective sees in the other a president and in himself a vice-president. The one that stays home, the 'vice president", seeks in the other someone to help him in the tasks of the house, and as a "vice-president' he realizes that he is only a laborer. This erroneous thought entraps us in the same thought as the result, we both torment our partner and ourselves. Our flare-ups keep us cagey, in order to confront the other as someone standing in opposition to us whom we must change. Of course, in this way we chase him even farther away. In a home, both are presidents. More important as president, however, is the woman. She is the president, and always will be, because she alone has the first word in the house, the children, the family and her husband. Her trap, though, is her enclosure in the house, the isolation that brings up thinking, that in turn bring insistence, thus generating the problems.

Another problem afflicting relationships is that both partners feel an injustice has been done to them. Indeed, most feel that they only offer and never take, where in fact, both take and forget to give.

Whatever the case, however, the real leader is the one that is plagued by the least level of disorder.

What I wish to advise people burdened with problems, either psychological or physical, is to create friendships with individuals that are stronger than you so that they drag you out and heal you so that you feel joy. Friendships are not created to suffer together, to pull each other to the problems but to help each other escape from the problems. This is why one of the friends must be stronger. The same happens with groups of people, associations: You must know that, if we are faced with a psychological problem (e.g. suffer from depression), we must seek from others what we ourselves lack, that is, we must seek to create friendships with people that have vitality and joie de vivre, so that, with their help we integrate again in society, and not create groups that set us apart and isolate us from our environment.

We have an opportunity henceforth, once we know this. To conclude, I remind you that all types are capable in a relationship to come to terms with the other once they have achieved conciliation with themselves.

What is pertinent is to fully erase the past that bedevils and burdens us, both good things and bad things. Yes, the good things as well because they are in the past and by keeping them we entrap ourselves in a fairytale. We miss out on the present, life itself.

We should never carry stuff over to today. We must live today! We live every moment!

Every day, before leaving work to return home, we should leave behind our problems. Before going to sleep, also, we must make a ledger of the day and throw off the problems we have amassed, so that every day should be the dawn of a new day.

If we do not do this, thoughts accumulate in us and create a mountain that slowly burdens us more and more, and as the mountain grows bigger, our feelings change. They become feelings of panic and pain, and there comes the moment we express this negativity, pain or panic to those around us because we blame them for creating it. The result is that we lock and isolate ourselves in our solitude. To be calm, we must uproot these feelings from within us, with a daily account. Not a ledger going back years but one going back moments!

Do we really have time for ourselves? Is our aim to change the others, or to rectify ourselves in order to be able to live harmoniously with them?

Does the pressure of thinking allow us to check what is right and what is wrong? No, we never saw what we gave, we only observed what we received in return and this annoys us. That which presses us we express it through the look in our face and then we articulate it in 'word'.

We must, at the end of the day, realize that what we have received is that which we gave, and at the same time, what we gave is what we had, because this is the cash flow of the human beings: one receives what one gives.

It is what we are that bothers us on the 'other', for, had we not had it, we would have not observed it on the other. Do you have meanness in your soul? You will observe mean people first of all, and they will irritate you. Are you evil? You will think all are evil. Are you good? You will deem all being good. It is the 'mind' that generates thoughts which opens our way to good and evil.

Solutions? They exist.

If you love yourself, you will love others and forgive people even for problems that are not yours. You will transcend them and not allow them to torment you for the rest of your life

BODY POSTURE OF EACH TYPE

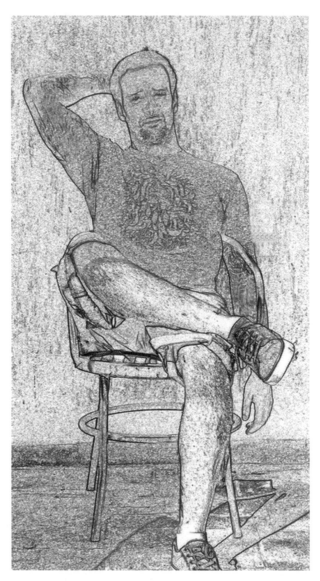

MALE A ♂

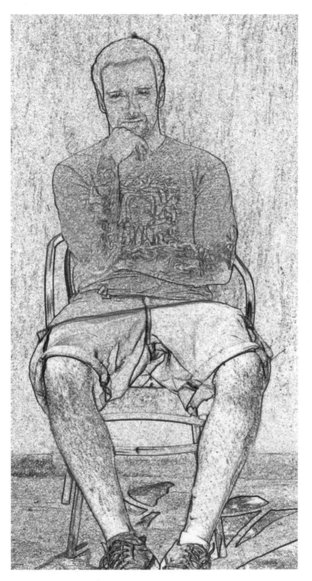

MALE A ♀

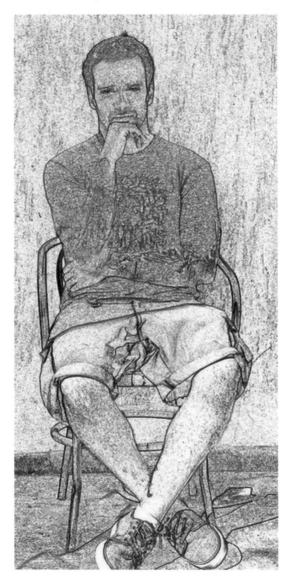

MALE B ♂

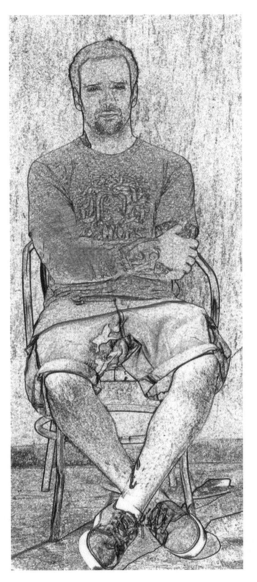

MALE B ♀

MALE C ♂

MALE C ♀

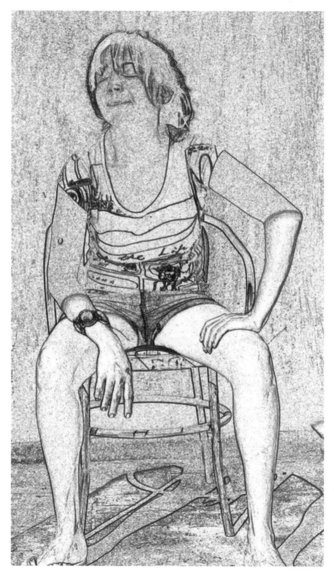

FEMALE A ♂

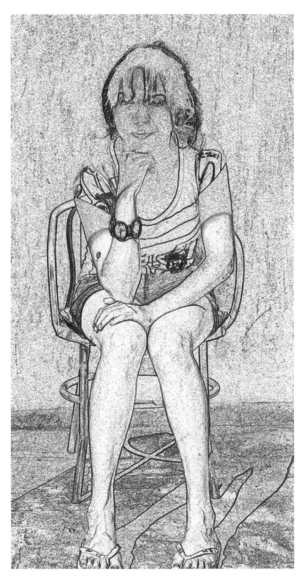

FEMALE A ♀

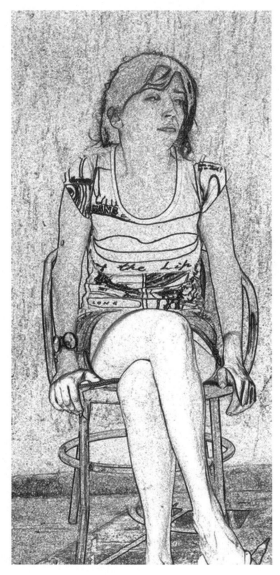

FEMALE B ♂

FEMALE B ♀

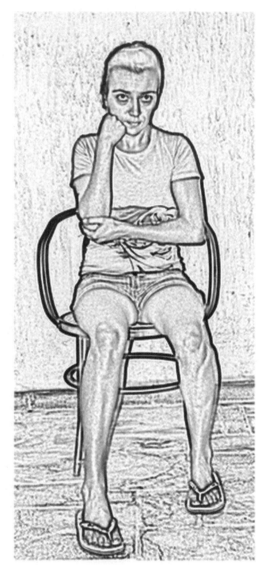

FEMALE C ♂

FEMALE C ♀

THE TOTAL HORMONAL DISORDER

Life is chemistry.
So is stress

Life, as perceived by our senses, is but movement and interactions – that is, relations of physical bodies.

The basic building block of the human body is the cell. Every cell in our body consists (up to 99%) of four elements: oxygen, hydrogen, carbon and nitrogen. We say that the cell is the basic structural unit of the human body because it is autonomous. It is born, pulsates, grows, reproduces, reacts to stimuli from the environment and dies. That is to say, it possesses all he characteristics of a living organism.

Our cells are organized in similar groups and create sets, (tissues, organs and systems), each of which has its own function and cooperates with the rest of the complicated systems of the body in order to support the various functions of our life. The interaction between tissues and organs takes place through a continuous, almost real-time exchange of information (once again we see how important information is), coordinated by our brain.

The brain also consists of cells, the so called nerve cells or neurons, and it is the main organ of the nervous system that communicates through the peripheral nerves and the spinal cord, sending information of their proper function.

This information is transmitted through the neurotransmitters which are chemical molecules transmitted through electric discharges wherever this is required in the body. The neurotransmitters interact in the body very quickly, usually between 1 and 10 thousandth of a second. The endocrine system reacts more slowly to the change of states and transmits information by secreting hormones created in the glands that constitute it.

Two of the most significant neurotransmitters are *serotonin and dopamine.*

The secretion of serotonin causes feelings of well-being, but it can also cause a sense of daydreaming, followed by hallucinations. Dopamine, on the other hand, causes intense feelings of alertness and pleasure.

The pituitary gland, at the base of our brain, controls the secretion of cortizole, the stress hormone. 'Stress' is a medical term borrowed from applied mechanics and signifies the concentration of tensions on a particular point on the surface.

'Stress' is used in engineering to increase the resistance of materials: using a hammer (at early stages of metallurgy) and then through modern means we introduce stress within steel (forged steel) in order to increase its load-bearing capacity compared to non-forged steel.

The so-called 'good stress' has a similar function in the human body. It helps to keep us in a condition of readiness to act, a situation that generally causes pleasant sentiments.

However, if stress is intense and permanent, the immune system suffers and our organs overload and we fall ill. Since, then, our hormones are easily secreted following the stimulus but if their influence stays on for some time, it is rather easy for the immune system to deteriorate.

The disorder

The data provided in this section could soon be given in a way that would help their immediate use by medical science. I was given the power to be able to *recognize and intuitively measure the total function - dysfunction of the human body,* something hitherto not possible through medical tests, but only through the gift of intuition.

I have already mentioned that during my stay in Germany, where I saw many patients and recognized their health problems, I have compiled a measuring scale – arbitrary as it were – in an effort to classify these problems so that I gain quicker and more accurate results, but also in order to have a quicker and more successful collaboration with the doctors. I have defined this scale from 1 to 100. By observing from which point on this scale the health problems start manifesting, I came to the conclusion that the higher the index rose on the scale the more serious the health problems were. However, besides the reactions that I could 'see' on the body of the patients, manifest were also the explosive behaviors that were certainly due to their psychological condition were also manifest. I named the hormonal function index the 'Total Hormonal Disorder'.

It is pertinent that I point out again that a 'disorder' refers to and measures the purely physical dysfunction caused by a psychological condition (anxiety, stress, acute sorrow etc.). I do not tire of stressing (no pun intended) that psychological condition and bodily functions are inextricably intertwined since one depends on the other. All diseases are psychosomatic and I am in a position to ascertain the precise cause of the problem and the time of its occurrence.

Doctors who support this work know and tell us that all the evident (from the point of view of research and study only) systems of the human body are linked to one another; one influences the other and both work together in order to produce and maintain the harmony we call 'health'. The pituitary system is made up of eight different glands that, controlled by the central gland (the pituitary gland which functions as an orchestra conductor) produce the hormones. Hormones are chemical substances that carry messages to the organs in the body in order to best coordinate, in each circumstance, bodily functions.

The pituitary gland is located in the brain that constitutes the operational center of the body. It functions as the receptor of all information in the form of electromagnetic energy (you will read more about this in the chapter 'The Cosmic influence on our Eating'.)

The human brain also controls our logical functions (it processes the information it receives from the environment through the senses and it forms a total picture of the entire human body at any given moment) just like the officers in command centers we have seen in films.

Through the nerve and the pituitary (hormonal) system the brain 'orders' the body to function properly, thus creating and maintaining a 'program' similar to those used in computers.

The proper functioning of every computer program depends on the accuracy of the data fed into the program. A friend of mine who is a computer nerd informed me that in the language of the old computers was a term, 'GIGO', an acronym that stood for 'garbage in, garbage out'.

Because the soul is expressed by the mind, and the mind is expressed by thoughts, it is the state of our soul that finally determines the state of our body. The longer we retain a thought in the mind, the more we give the wrong signals to the neurotransmitters, thus allowing the disorder to rise (the 'garbage' of the computers).

Thoughts that are retained and repeated become a fixation. Fixations create agitation that leads us down the road of isolation, pain and disease.

As long as the body is in an active state and in motion, the brain automatically gives orders, and the body produces and sends to the organs the elements required for its self-preservation. When the body in not in action, the pains are more acute because the thought is being sent somewhere else and is preoccupying the mind. The pituitary gland is blocked and the body is not properly fed information. The functioning of the self-therapeutic mechanism of the body is interrupted.

When we have proper control of our thoughts, we are in a position then to solve the problems we are facing. The psychological blockage, that is our excessive ego, is what traps us and pressures us to react explosively, resulting in our poisoning both soul and body. Health or sickness have a direct relationship to the total functioning of chemical body secretions and depend on their proportion and interaction.

When we develop an infection, the way we treat it is crucial. If we stay in bed, it will last for a fortnight.

If we stay on our feet it will not last at all!

This disorder manifests itself with an increase of the speed of the pulsed cytokinesis that normally should not exceed 7,4 Hz. Any gland functioning at a speed faster than 44 Hz will develop cancer. The friction between cells at the speed of 7,4 Hz is the one that keeps the temperature of our body at 37°C. When higher speeds occur at a particular gland (depending on the sensitivity of each of the three types), excessive local heating is produced resulting gradually in the creation of a small tumor. Depending on the type and the temperament of each, this is the point where an increase in the speed of the pulsed cytokinesis occurs. For example, to a type A woman the first increase in speed occurs at a gland in the right breast, while for a type C woman, the left breast will be affected.

I will give you now the particular figures of the disorder that reveal the functional level of our body, as I 'see' it and measure it.

Let us start with children, where the highest 'normal' disorder in my scale ranges from 7-10 and by the age of 18 it may reach 17-20.

With adults, the body functions normally and no

problem occurs when the disorder is maintained from 24 to 28. From 30-40, the body starts to dysfunction, without, though, showing any noticeable problems. Cysts start appearing after 40. (Between 30-40, men in particular are susceptible to a disorder of the stomach and the esophagus, with the possible occurrence of gastro-esophageal reflux and duodenum ulcer,.)

From 40 to 43 the body shows inflammations, fistulas, fissures and hemorrhoids.

Around 43-45 there occur polyps, lipomas, varicocele (on the man), fissures, nodules, adenomas, and to the women fibroids that increase in size as the disorder advances.

Above 50, and pending the type of the person and one's personal sensitivities, things become more explosive. For example, above 53 types, A may suffer a stroke, while types B and C may suffer a heart attack.

When the disorder reaches beyond 54, the brain cannot distinguish between joy and sorrow, and the happy events in life may have the same effects as the sad ones do.

Beyond 60, if the disorder remains at these high levels for long, cancer will start to develop, and at the level of 64 it may also be diagnosed by orthodox medicine. This is an observation holding true for all types. When the disorder reaches 75 a metastasis occurs. Above 80 we see a second metastasis. Higher than 90, the body is extremely weakened, and it is very difficult for it to recover.

However, there are cases of high level disorders at 130, like a lady that suffered from metastatic cancer but who is still with us after receiving our help.

The disorder advances when repeated sorrows and continued stress are around and we fail to rid ourselves of them. We have already said that stress may be necessary at some degree, as it motivates us and pushes us to achieve our goals. What is harmful is when the stress is permanent. Then, when the tension becomes a permanent situation, we do not allow ourselves to be calm and find a balance.

Our body has the capacity to withstand sadness. When the onslaught subsides, we allow it to function with harmony and joy. It is the accumulation of sorrow and the continuous pain that 'breaks' our natural function and our self-healing capacity. Then, the disorder gradually advances and we are exposed to various illnesses.

When, after an illness occurs, the disorder index subsides to levels lower than 40. then, our body has the capacity to hear itself.

A body at normal disorder levels needs at least six years of continuous emotional abuse in order for the disorder to reach levels above 60 and for cancer to appear.

When the disorder has once reached high levels, although with my help this may be decreased to normal, the "road uphill" remains open and every new sorrow in the next 18-24 months may have multiple impacts on the increase of the disorder.

In general, we may say that man and woman 'go together' when the disorder goes beyond 40, with the women showing more sensitivity to the gynecological issues and man to the intestine.

It seems as if types A, B or C, are trapped in their brain's 'cassette'. Yet, is it our skeletal structure that will determine our quotidian attitude and advancement, or are we put our soul ahead of the game, – now that we know about the limitations and capacities of our type - in order to live every moment in a more positive way?

By offering to humanity, through science, knowledge and the articulation of this disorder index – that many distinguished doctors and researchers who have worked with me methodically try to ascertain, understand, systematize, measure and scientifically use in research centers – I hope that science and, by extension, mankind will benefit from it.

Regarding disorders, in general, we could say that the tendency of every body is to return to normal, when the event that temporarily raises the disorder is overcome. Thus, we should not worry excessively when we are faced with adversity. We should face it in the best possible way and then say goodbye to it.

Let us 'rid ourselves' of the garbage and not allow ourselves project negativity (pain, sorrow, and feeling of injustice) and let this negativity determine our reactions, poisoning thus our body and behavior. Let us be open to the joys of life. All around us, there is a mechanism surreptitiously 'robbing' us of our time with useless, talkative information, empty gossiping and pointless chatter that only result in taking us away from our inner reality, from the world of our depth.

All these prompt us to have and to exhibit qualities, quantities, material goods, possessions that can be measured and exhibited in order that they give us value and elevate our ego.

Instead of simply *pursuing* what to have, let us pursue what *to be*.

Let us accept the energy we receive from the sun as love, because it is the love of God for His creation. Let us allow the information, the thread of life, to enter our minds, without us tormenting it, without tiring ourselves with continuous and pointless thoughts, blocking in the end the balanced functioning or our body. Let us not allow bad, anxious thinking to block the love that is directed towards us to enter us.

When we go to sleep nurturing bad thoughts, we are going to have a bad sleep, our sleep will not relax us, and we will wake up in a bad mood that will stay with us for the rest of the day. "You made your bed now lay in it", says a well-known proverb. There is much literal truth in this case.

Therefore, make, a ledger of your daily activities and of all that has happened and throw away what is redundant, in order to help your balance and preserve yourself. Do not allow your thoughts to rob you of love.

CONCEPTION AND PREGNANCY

Genetics is the science that examines the way in which the biological and morphological features and traits are passed from the parents to the offspring.

The genetic information that determines the characteristics of a new body obeys certain biological rules.

The characteristics of the foetus are transferred through the genes that are found in the chromosomes of the cells of the two parents.

As I have mentioned earlier, I have 'seen' that the dominant gene with regards to the determination of the type of the new man that is being created is one, and comes from the parent that during conception presents the highest defense, and consequently, the lowest disorder. From the parent, that is, that, during conception, was at the best physical condition.

It is amazing, resulting from the infinite wisdom of

nature, that the foetus will take the dominant gene during conception regarding its type, from the parent that at this time, of conception, had the highest defense and the smallest disorder. The chromosomes of this parent are healthier, pulsate more vibrantly at a higher frequency and multiply faster, undertaking thus to fashion the skeleton of the foetus. The child's type originates from the parent who was at the best physical condition during conception; therefore it is his type that is dominant to the benefit of the baby, the new life.

For three days after conception, a battle takes place between the 46 chromosomes   (23 from the man and 23 from the woman) vying for the domination of the strongest. The domination of the strongest will determine the skeleton type of the foetus, termed 'conception', and it is then that conception is completed and the growth of the foetus begins.

Until the sixth week, the foetus takes part of the mother's body, and its cells pulsate in the same frequency as the mother's body. On the sixth week the foetus begins to seek the independence of its function, its own soul, its own pulse, as it has already completed the creation of the three million stem cells that are necessary for it to become autonomous.

This number signals the beginning of the new life, as the new body begins to attract the soul. This traction is the first 'entry' of the soul in the foetus, and causes the first frisk that the mother feels. This battle lasts for three days until the foetus becomes autonomous from the refusal of the mother's cells to allow it to assume its own cell pulsating movement, so that its heart beats autonomously.

Until it becomes seven months and one week old, the foetus' cells cannot autonomously pulsate but only if aided by the mother. If the baby is born prematurely, on the seventh month and one week, it does not face the danger of dying, as its weight is so small that, with the help of the incubator it is capable to vibrate its own cells and survive. There is this great chance of survival because the skeletal construction has been completed and at this time the mother relaxes a little, leaving to the baby some autonomy.

During the eighth month, in contrary, there begins the speedier production of cells from the part of the mother, in order for the speedy completion of the development of the child's body, and in case of a premature birth it is more difficult for the child, but also the mother to survive. This is due to the fact that the child, for its part, is unable to pulsate by itself the greater number of its cells and the mother's body is in a hyperactive state and may suffer hemorrhages.

The importance of disorder during conception

We shall engage now more thoroughly with women's disorder and how this affects the period cycle and the capacity to conceive, but also how it burdens the other organs of her body.

Nature's wisdom sees to that, when the disorder is over 25, the conception is next to impossible because the child, if the disorder index does not subside, will be born with a health problem.

Yet, clinically there are no pathological indications. Almost all of us have encountered such examples of totally normal and healthy couples, as shown in their medical examinations, who, however, cannot conceive children. Are they really 'normal' and 'healthy'? Science did not, hitherto, know of the 'disorder' factor and its importance in the overall health of man.

A body that shows a disorder level up to 25 functions normally. From 25 to 27 pregnancies can only be achieved through IVF and from 27 to 40, women find difficulties in conceiving. But even if they do, they will most probably lose the baby in the first month.

An indication to young women that have an increased disorder (from 28 to 40) is the pains they feel during their period, the appearance of bigger or lesser hemorrhaging than normal and low time deviations, from 2-3 days in the cycle.

At these levels of disorder, that is, up to 40, a conception of twins or triplets may occur. The mother's body in this case goes through an accelerated production of cells in order to avoid the birth of one child with serious problems; thus, she proceeds to the production of more!

Multiple gestations, therefore, is the result of high hormonal disorder. Benefits which originate from a problem!

In addition, we may also remark that only a woman of type C can bear twins or triplets through a normal conception. When it comes to the multiple gestation, inheritance only concerns women in the same family that inherit type C either from the father or the mother from generation to generation. Women of another type may have a multiple gestation exclusively through IVF.

The body of types A and B women that show disorder levels higher than 30 loses the child, whilst (at a percentage of 80%) a woman of type C showing the same disorder will keep it.

If the partner of a woman type C with the same disorder is an A type and the child inherits the dominant gene from him, the problem bound to occur is of a motor or neurological nature: spasticity, schizophrenia, epilepsy fits (seizures) etc.

If, now, the child's father is of B type and the mother's disorder is high, the child may have the Down syndrome, while if the disorder is at a lower level there may occur autism, deafness-muteness, and other disorders in hearing or speech.

Finally, if the father is of type C and the child has inherited the dominant gene from him, it may be born without extremities or without some organs and show spastic mobility.

When both mother and father are of type C, they both bear the same stigma, the same 'heritage' of anemia. This, in combination with the disorder causes teratogenicity. In those cases where the child has received the gene from a mother of type C with a high disorder, the result is children with severe problems in blood circulation or the urological system. The above statements are confirmed through thousands of records from 2003 until today. All infants that showed some serious problem were from type C mothers, because only a type C mother is able to conceive, gestate and give birth to a child even when she has an disorder higher than 35.

During pregnancy, the body needs to produce large quantities of calcium for the formation of the baby's skeleton, and for this purpose nature has equipped the female body with a strong mechanism for calcium production. This mechanism can produce far larger quantities of calcium than the male body. For this reason, only women show the sensitivities and exhibit calcium fluctuations when under a high hormonal disorder, resulting to problems in the deposition of calcium to the joints.

Specifically, women of type C, because of their intolerance to lactose (that is used by the body for the production of calcium), have a greater problem in producing calcium needed for the growth of the child's skeleton. And since they are the only women that can keep foetus while having a higher disorder, and since their body cannot produce the correct quantities of calcium, the baby will have congenital problems of the spinal column.

Whatever serious problem a child show up to his 29th year (cancer or diabetes, for example) is clearly due to the period of gestation during which skeleton is formed. Wherever the skeleton was not properly formed, the person shows this sensitivity.

The dysfunction of the neck – brain causes the problem. With the first psychological pressure during pregnancy, because the period of the formation of the skeleton is brief, the missing structural elements of the new body cause abnormalities in the skeletal construction of the neck and the cerebellum. The result is a loosening of the spinal column neurons of the neck that cannot constrict the vertebrae together so that the child can keep its balance and walk. Scoliosis is created and the spinal column cannot assume its correct posture. There occur, then, mobility problems.

I point out that all this is caused when the mother, during pregnancy, withdraws to herself and thoughts take hold of her mind. It is easy for thoughts to become fixations, resulting in poisoning the body of the mother and, by extension, of the child that is gestated.

It is, then, obvious for what particular reason the prenatal education of the mother is so important.

The health of our mind and body
is structured before birth*

Modern science considers the prenatal stage, the period from conception to birth, to be of fundamental importance for the health, mental balance and mental development of man throughout his life. This period before birth – the roots of life – should be experienced by the fetus or by the mother and father (the emotions of the father are transferred to the mother) with joy, pride, love for the child and harmony. This period has direct consequences on the health of the body and mind of the unborn child, but also on the adult this child is going to develop into, on his ability to love

---

(Mrs. Ioanna Mari, psychologist, writer, chairman of the Greek Society of Prenatal Education and the International Federation of Prenatal Education, State Councilor, founding member of our Non-profit Organization and dear friend, offers voluntarily valuable information and prevention in this field. The present chapter hinges upon her specialization and interests, and I thank her warmly for preparing this text.)

himself, his fellow people, the environment, to live life with joy and develop his talents and intelligence.

In all domains of medicine we see all the more often the undertaking of research, which links diseases with characteristics of the personality of the child and the adult with factors that affected the prenatal or perinatal stage. The research proves that most diseases and severe dysfunctions have their roots in the intrauterine life.

Fortunately, the same applies for the good health and the talents of the child and the adult.

The foundations of a baby's entire body and indeed of its major organs (the brain, the heart, the liver) and all its systems (nervous, circulatory, parasympathetic, digestive, muscular, skeletal) are laid from the time the very first zygote cell is created to the time it is born. The proper development of the organs or systems depends on the materials (physical, mental, spiritual) that will be offered to it by the father and the mother during conception, and subsequently, mainly by the mother – with the contribution of the father and the environment – during the nine months of its intrauterine life.

In these nine months, the foundations of its mental and spiritual qualities, its inclinations and its intelligence are laid through the most powerful, since they are the first, impressions on its cellular memory of thoughts, emotions, sense impressions, experiences of the mother, and, through her, of the father and the familial environment.

• For nine months, the child is formed from the mother's blood circulation of the placenta. It is important that the mother's blood be clean – free of toxins and rich in the requisite ingredients, through a balanced and healthy diet.

Many researches refer to the influence of diet to the health of the child and, subsequently, the adult.

For example, research that took place in Holland in winter of 1944-45, when pregnant women were deprived of food in the first six months of their pregnancy, came to the conclusion that this deprivation was linked to obesity, serious antisocial behavior or the onset of schizophrenia to the child or adult.

The diet of a pregnant woman must contain proteins, carbohydrates, fatty acids and all the necessary minerals and vitamins. It has been proven that the lack of, say, zinc in the mother's diet, due to chemical fertilizers in the food and her intense anxiety, constitutes a cause for the appearance of schizophrenia in adolescence and diabetes in middle age.

• The emotional state of the pregnant woman influences the growth of the baby, the child and the adult. Thoughts, emotions, alternating impressions and experiences of the pregnant woman affect her hormonal system.

Thus, when the pregnant woman is sad, fearful or pessimistic, hormones like adrenaline, cortisones and catecholamine are secreted in her bloodstream, reach through the placenta the blood circulation of the baby and disrupt its proper growth. On the contrary, joy, hope, optimism and the mother's love cause the secretion of endorphins and oxytocin, the love hormone, and as these beneficial hormones are flushed through the mother's blood stream in the baby's body, they promote its healthy growth. They also instill in the baby the same emotional states that, if repeated, the baby will grow up into an adult with a happy, enthusiastic and optimistic personality.

The emotional disturbances in the mother during pregnancy constitute high risk factors for the manifestation of youth criminal behavior. In

Finland, 167 children that had lost their father during pregnancy and 168 children whose father died during the first year of their life were studied for a period of 35 years. Both groups grew up without a father. Yet, only the children who had experienced their mother's deep grief and bereavement in the womb developed criminal behavior later.

We need to point out here that eclampsia appears to be caused by oxidation due to anxiety.

Severe repercussions also follow from the rejection of the pregnancy by mother and father. Finnish research has shown that schizophrenia is caused by the rejection of the child by the pregnant woman.

• The influence of mother's emotions, ideas, temperament and experiences on the baby is also of a genetic nature. This, because the thoughts, emotions and experiences of the pregnant mother are "information" that has been recorded in the cellular memory of the baby and constitutes the first imprint, the beginnings of tomorrow's personality, its inclinations and talents, particularities, its life pattern.

If, what comes from the mother and the father is positive, it creates new positive inscriptions, neutralizes (leaves mute) all the old negative inscriptions and activates new ones. The opposite happens with the negative emotions and unpleasant thoughts of the mother.

All new knowledge on the science of genetics is very important; it shows the great opportunity future parents have to give birth to physically and emotionally healthy babies.

Science teaches that the baby is a rational, conscious being from the first moment of fertilization of the ovum by the sperm. Whatever the mother thinks, feels or experiences, is automatically conveyed to the baby.

During the nine months of pregnancy, the future parents have the opportunity, as the child interacts exclusively with the mother and, indirectly through her with the father, to form a permanent basis for the development of its body. Through their thoughts and visions, their love and constructive experiences they can imprint in the baby's cellular memory good character, as well as the laws of a harmonious, honest, happy and optimistic life.

This positive influence is the most precious gift to their baby in its entire life.

The Baby's Senses

The human sensory organs are not like a mechanism that can function only after the completion of its construction. According to Dr Gerald Guther, in a developing human body the formation of the organs and their function proceed in tandem. The baby's sensory organs begin to function from the moment they are formed.

The baby possesses the sense of touch. It can feel the touch of the mother or the father over the belly, and moves its entire body to reach their hand. This caress fills it with a sense of security and bliss. The Dutch scientist Franz Veldman developed the scientific approach of *'haptonomy'* (laws of touch) that is now taught to the students of medicine.

It has the sense and beginning of smell. Sweet tastes in the mother's food and her sweet disposition that sweetens her liquids in the womb, please it! On the contrary, her bitterness and the bitter substances in her food repulse it! It has been observed that in these circumstances the baby makes grimaces of displeasure. In fact, his mother's choices determine his future preferences.

Above all, the baby **hears**: the heartbeat, the rhythm of walking, the voice of the mother, the sounds in the environment, the music! In this way, rhythm and melody, the love for speech and music are imprinted in the baby's brain.

The baby loves soft classical music, that pays heed to the rhythm of the body, particularly Mozart's music, Vivaldi, Greek folk and Byzantine music and gets disturbed by modern noisy music*.

_____

(The Japanese scientist Masaru Emoto, in his book The Secret Message of the Water, explains the property of the water to receive and record sounds, music, images, feelings, words and messages from the environment, and to create patterns in its crystals when it freezes. So he took photos of water samples that were saturated with the beautiful music of Mozart (Symphony 40) or from the phrases, "I love you", "Thank you", "I am grateful to you". Then he saw in its crystals magnificent, harmonious shapes and colors. On the contrary, shapeless, non-elegant patterns appeared in the water that was saturated with heavy metal music or with the phrases "I hate you", "You are an idiot". Is it perhaps the positive and negative influences of the environment on the water another explanation of the influence the mother and the father have on the fetus? Let us not forget that the fetus is more than ninety percent water, and an adult around 70-75 percent.)

The fetus memorizes the music it hears. It learns the mother tongue (language of the womb) as it listens to the mother's voice. The person that, as a baby, has listened to speech and music in the womb will become an eloquent adult and will show a highly developed skill in learning and communicating. Yehudi Menuhin, Olivier Messsian and A. Rubinstein stated that they owed their musical talent to their mother who used to play or listened to music during pregnancy! Also, the American conductor Boris Brott used to say that he knew the cello part that his mother was studying during her pregnancy off by heart!

Musical education of the child must begin before birth. Mothers educators that spoke clearly and accurately tell us how their children spoke early and with a rich vocabulary and showed high academic performance in school. Speech and music multiply the synapses of the brain and strengthen the nervous system, laying the foundation for eloquence and high intelligence.

Vision, the need for light, is less developed in the womb. Yet, many incidents reveal that the baby is aware – we do not know how – of the external environment.

I relate some relevant experiences of mothers: a mother narrated how, when she was pregnant, slipped and fell from the stairs of her house, thankfully with no consequences for the baby. After the birth, her baby cried uncontrollably every time they passed by the staircase.

A young lady that was watching a TV program on prenatal education phoned to say that she was fearful of men and always nurtured the fear that her father would hit her, although he had never touched her. Her mother revealed what had caused that fear, explaining to her that her husband, when she was pregnant to this daughter, had beaten her up. The girl always knew.

Life is still a mystery.

THE MENTAL EXPERIENCES OF THE BABY

The baby shares the **emotions** and feels the **love** of its mother and father, and hence it is blissful. On the contrary, their indifference or displeasure for its birth or the lack of a desire to see it born is its most tragic experiences that will trouble it for the rest of its life.

Dr Thomas Verny, a psychiatrist from Toronto, maintains that in order for man to feel and show the love and sympathy to his fellow people and enjoy perfect mental health he must have received the love of the mother and father from the beginning of his life, since his conception.

"The love towards the unborn baby is the most significant factor for the development of synapses in its brain, and therefore for the creation of a human being that is bright and of quality", he maintains.

Scientists, psychologists and psychiatrists have shown the profound significance of the emotional bond that the mother creates and maintains with the child and his future.

Adding the studies of his colleagues to his, Dr Thomas Verny, tells us: "The love that a mother feels for her child, the thoughts she has for it, the quality of communication she maintains with it, all have a decisive influence on its physical formation, the outline of its personality and the dispositions of its character."

Yet, a study of 500 women showed that one third of them did not think at all about the baby they carried in their womb, either because pregnancy was unwanted or because they believed that nature works through them and they did not need to do anything to cooperate with it. The children they brought to life weighed less than normal, and showed more frequent and more severe nervous and digestive disorders than other children. They cried a lot and during their first years of their lives they showed difficulties in adapting to others and to life in general.

Professor A. Fedor-Feybergh of the University of Stockholm mentions the case of young Christina, who, since birth refused to take her mother's breast, but she eagerly turned to the bottle offered to her or grasped the breast of another woman and nursed hungrily. The professor had the intuition to ask the mother:

"Lady, did you really want to have this child?"

"No", was the answer. 'I wanted to to have an abortion, but my husband wanted the child, so I kept her".

No doubt, the child sensed the mother's rejection and returned it.

An example of a long term damage inflicted to an adult is mentioned by the German researcher Paul Blick, pioneer in hypnotherapy. One day, he received a patient who complained for severe bouts of anxiety, followed by hot flushes". In order to discover the causes, Dr Blick subjected him to hypnotherapy. The patient began to investigate the months preceding his birth, remembering and relating specific events, until the moment he reached the seven month. Then, his voice broke and he was overwhelmed with panic. Obviously he had reached the point of the cause of his problem. He was complaining that he was hot and greatly fearful. Why? His mother gave the answer.

In a long and anguished discussion with the doctor she confessed that during the seventh month she tried to abort the child by having very hot baths.

The baby can also sense the mother's **thoughts**.

The images, thoughts and ideas that the mother nurtures in her, replenished with her emotions, particularly those relating to the child, influence it, inform it.

The impact of the mother's thoughts to the baby has been studied by the French university researcher Marie Claire Bysnell, who said: "The baby reacts to both the speech and the thoughts of the mother, when these thoughts have clarity and intensity". The images and thoughts about the child imprint impressions and form its existence.

The new discoveries brought about a revolution regarding the critical role of the future parents and their great capacity to build the future of the child, thus laying the foundations of its health from an early age and structuring positively the power of its soul!

A true pedagogue makes sure that new life grows well. This is easier and more effective, than trying later to straighten a bent tree.

Prenatal education will bring enormous improvement to the new generation (eugenics).

Ancient Greek care
for eugenics

Do we think this knowledge to be novel? *It may be novel for science, but ancient Greek philosophy and modern Greek tradition were well aware of it for centuries.*

In ancient Greece, the primary care of the city was to guide couples to give birth to healthy and beautiful offspring.

Iamblichus, in his work Life of Pythagoras points out that, according to Pythagoras' teaching, parents should not neglect their duty to raise good and honorable children. He also commented on the indifference that parents show towards their newly born by contrasting it with the great care that animal lovers show when their beloved horse, dog or bird is about to breed.

Plato, in his Laws, advises young people to take care of their health, particularly during the period of childbearing, taking precautions not to indulge in violent or unjust acts because, as he maintained, such behaviors are instilled into the bodies and souls of the children they will bring to this world. In particular, pregnant women, according to Plato, must live calmly and happily, avoiding brawls and sadness.

Aristotle, in his Politics, agrees with Plato in what he regards peacefulness during pregnancy, and compares the pregnant woman with the earth and the babies with the sprouts that draw life from the soil.

It was compulsory for all married Greek women in antiquity to participate in the Thesmophoria, an initiation festival celebrating Demeter, goddess of fertility and matron goddess of women that were about to experience maternity and kalligeneia, the ability to obtain healthy and beautiful offspring.

Ancient Greek women were fully aware of their responsibility for the quality of the children they brought to this world. Aristophanes, in Thesmophoriazousai, suggests that honors and facilities should be offered to women that have brought to life sons who proved to be useful to the city.

Ten simple rules for future parents

If the couple wonders how to prepare the creation of a new life, here are some simple but particularly dynamic rules.

1. Conception with love

Science claims that "the mental condition of the couple at the time of conception, if bad, creates a particularly negative climate for the development of the baby that may manifest itself in a congenital anomaly". It encourages avoiding conception during periods of adverse mental condition of the lovers (announcement at the 16th PanHellenic Congress of Pediatric Surgery).

During conception the genetic plan for the new life is laid out. This plan, that is the DNA of the child, is intimately linked to the thoughts, emotions and the attitude of the couple during their union.

An attitude of admiration, respect and love creates a filter through which the best qualities of one's ancestors are expressed in the first DNA of the new existence; a selection from 7 generations of ancestors from the paternal line and 7 generations of ancestors from the maternal line!

"The selection of the genetic material depends on the way the couple live their life before conception and during pregnancy; it depends on the quality of their love for one another", maintains the geneticist Dr B. Lipton.

Joy, exultation, admiration, deep love and tenderness in their relationship before and during conception, that is, a noble physical, mental, spiritual and also sexual communication of the couple, constitute the necessary framework for the manifestation of important talents in the new existence that is incarnated through them.

The young people who love each other and decide to create a family must know that this act of love can produce marvelous results if experienced in exultation, tenderness and enthusiasm. And they have to be prepared to experience something 'great' in soul and light in order to attract a 'great' luminous soul.

To this 'great soul', in the coming nine months, they have to offer the possibility of expression, that is, the possibility of the manifestation of all its talents. And they will do so by ensuring that they will live with joy and pride for the new life. They must ensure that the body and soul of the new life is formed in the most harmonious way (epigenetics).

If during conception the couple is the architects that compose the plan of the new existence, the pregnant woman is the builder that will erect the whole edifice, putting in all the material and work. And just like a builder who has the ability to improve the plan, to straighten a badly shaped room, to open larger windows, to use better materials, the pregnant woman will also improve the plan of the new existence with her great formative power. She will be participating in the formation of the genetic capital (epigenetics), of what is most refined and developed, awakening the noblest emotions, creating the opportunity for synaptogenesis and myelinosis in more brain areas of the fetus.

The specialists also advise:
a) Abstinence from sex for many days in order to strengthen the male genetic material,
b) Morning sunbathing for both the man and the woman for therapy of the fallopian tubes and strengthening of their genetic system. It is a simple, but necessary preparation for conception.

The creative power of the mother is never ending, but always with the father next to her.

2. Relaxation of the pregnant woman and healthy life

Early sleep is recommended, because night sleep is more rejuvenating. No alcohol, no psychotropic substances, no cigarettes and chemical drinks, and drugs only with the doctor's prescription. According to extended medical research, all the above constitute causes for teratogenesis and they must be absolutely avoided. Furthermore, the pregnant woman must relax during the day, having some moments of peace and serenity combined with making small wishes for her baby.

3. Deep breaths

It is recommended that the mother take deep breaths in tree-planted areas, many times during the day, for the better oxidization of the blood and brain of both the mother and the baby.

4. Proper nutrition of the pregnant woman

Pregnant women, but also couples who wish to have a baby, should prefer live, fresh food, fruit and vegetables, green salads (spinach, lettuce, cabbage), cereal, potatoes, olive oil (added to the food after boiling), raw nuts (almonds for calcium, walnuts for Omega-3 fatty acids), brown bread, honey instead of sugar and yogurt instead of milk, as this is more easily digested than milk.

It is also good for the mother to consume fish two to three times a week, as fish is rich in Omega-3 fatty acids and necessary for the development of a "bigger brain". Fish is far more beneficial than meat, which today is loaded with toxins.

5. Internal peace and enthusiasm

The mother should contemplate the great honor of being a mother and offering to the world a valuable, creative existence. She should think warmly about the arrival of her child daily.

If there are difficulties in the life of the couple, they should tell their child about them and assure it of their love. This micro-climate of love and joy will neutralize the poisons of the difficulties. "The love of parents is the best shield against the adversities of life for the child", claims Dr Thomas Verny.

6. Close to nature and beauty, light and colors

Pregnant women should admire the beauty of the flowers, the trees, the sea, the mountains, the sky and the sun. She should admire the splendors of spring, the rising of the sun, the starry sky and the changing of the seasons.

"Let her admire the light of the sun and let her wish that her child has the bright sun for wisdom, its warmth for kindness and love in his heart, and its strength for health and vigor in his life" (a saying from the Greek island of Karpathos). The contact with the sun strengthens the body of the pregnant woman and the child and instills virtues to its soul. If she goes out in the morning sun, she should admire the colors everywhere. Every color will bring to her and her child its health-giving properties.

7. The love of the parents towards the future baby

According to scientific research, the acceptance of pregnancy and the expression of love from the father constitute an irreplaceable basis, the foundation of the baby's future health and intelligence, its joy for life and its capacity to love itself and others. The communication of the parents with the child, by caressing the belly, through speech, thought and emotion constitutes an essential part of the prenatal treatment. The love expressed daily by the father and the mother creates people that are bright, sociable and happy.

8. Envisaging, wishes for the child

The images in the mother's as well as the father's imagination create impressions that will guide the child later in life. The ancient Greeks had already observed that the child resembles the pictures that the mother used to look at or entertain in her imagination during conception and pregnancy.

The Stoics maintained that children resemble those that the pregnant woman used to see or bring to mind during pregnancy.

According to Empedocles women often fell in love with heroes or gods and gave birth to children that looked like them.

The couple should admire the virtues of great people. They should envisage the light of wisdom, the warmth of kindness and love, and the power of life, health and creativity.

9. Speech and music

Parents should talk to the child. The mother should get used to reading aloud, reciting positive texts, inspirational poems, with a clear, loud voice. Thus, as the child will be exposed to the clarity and richness of the sounds, it will later show an increased capacity for speech and love for communication. Equally, the couple should listen to music together, Mozart's incomparable music and also Vivaldi, pre-classical composers, the great choral works, the proud and joyful pieces of folk tradition, as well as quality modern and Byzantine music.

It has been proven that children of musicians or children of teachers and lawyers, who, because of their profession, spoke with clear and loud voice during pregnancy, have a natural ability for speech and communication; they start to speak at an early age and they have rich vocabulary. The brain centers for speech and music need these prenatal experiences for their full development.

10. Contact during pregnancy and breastfeeding

And when the blessed moment of birth arrives, the mother should place the baby on her body, to feel her warmth. The father should participate in the joy of birth.

She should breastfeed the baby immediately. "The child must start breastfeeding within half an hour from birth. At that time, it knows how to breastfeed instinctively, but later it must learn", claims Dr M. Odent.

The first milk and the warmth of the mother and father are the warmest welcoming, the basis for immunization and health, security and socialization, and a true source of life! The mother should breastfeed the baby feeling with the same love she felt during pregnancy. Her thoughts will have been imprinted in its cellular memory. The bond will be unbreakable if the child has breastfed consciously.

Even if the parents follow only some of the above, they will have great results!

BIBLIOGRAPHY/REFERENCES

In writing this article, information was used from the following:

Gouni Ol., Welcome, 2009.
Kafkalidis Ath., Dr, The knowledge of the Womb, ed. Olkos, Athens, 1980.
Kafkalidis Ath., Dr, The Power of the Womb and Subjective Truth, ed. Eleftheros
        Typos, Athens, 1987.
.Mari, I., Eugenics-Prenatal Education, The education of the Child begins at
        Conception, ed. Pyrinos Kosmos, Athens 2004.
Minutes of world conferences, seminars of prenatal education.
Bertin, M.A., The natural prenatal education, a hope for the child, the family, the
        society. Hellenic Society of Prenatal Education, Athens, 2008.
Huther G.., Weser In., The Secret of the First Nine Months, ed. Polytropo, 2008.

Janus L., The Nine Months that Influence our Life, ed. Dioptra, Athens, 2008.

Lind, Neuman, Music in the Beginning of Life, Reymondos, Athens, 1987.

Odent M., Dr, The Renaissance, Athens, 1991

Odent M., Dr, The Scientification of Love

Odent M., Dr, The Primal Health, in Verny Th., & Kelly J., The Secret Life of the

Unborn Child, New York, 1981

Relier J.P. Pr., L aimer avant qu il naisse, ed. Laffont, Paris, 1993.

Tomatis A.A., Dr, Nine Months in Paradise, Athens, 2000.

THE COSMIC INFLUENCE ON OUR NUTRITION

The role of the pituitary gland is known to medicine. What is not yet known is that the pituitary gland performs the biggest and most important function in the human body. It receives energy and through it gets information. At the same time, it emits electromagnetic energy through the neurotransmitters, and thus chemical substances necessary for the body functioning are secreted. These substances create, depending on the situation, tension or relaxation. As the tension grows more intense, the more incomplete the information we get. And as we do not receive information, our body is weakened.

The pituitary gland is connected to the thymus gland that gives the order. It is located on the highest point of the mediastinum, behind the sternum, and is intimately linked with the heartbeat.

We often say, without giving it some serious thought, that we too are part of the universe, a part of our planetary system. What is not known is the extent that our everydayness is affected because of this, that, as it were, we are part of the Whole.

The human brain is the most complicated computational system we know: 1.300-1.500 gr. of gelatinous tissue comprising 100 billion neurons (as many as the stars in our galaxy) each of which creates thousands of synapses with adjacent neurons. It is built in the image of the Universe, a small universe within the large.

It is the center of reason, and as we have said, it accommodates our logic, which we control ourselves. Our logic was given to us so that we can consciously enjoy our earthly paradise. It produces the emotions that change with incredible speed, because they move with the speed of thought, which is the greatest speed in the universe.

Up to now, we knew that there are nine planets in our planetary system. Recently (1995) the astronomers discovered a tenth planet of our planetary system. In fact there are twelve planets, three of which have moved to a distance, however without having left our planetary system completely. They are far enough so that they do not affect our bodies, because the information they emit does not reach our brain. The planets affect our disorder, reflecting, as it were, the energy emitted by the sun and carrying information from and to the entire planetary system, and also to us. The trajectory of the planets constantly changes their distance from the Earth, with the result that our emotions are affected, because the planet closest to us, with the elements it contains, affects us more than the more remote ones.

The information that reaches our brain affects the pituitary gland, which is activated electromagnetically, receiving information related to the material elements (magnesium, iron, calcium, manganese etc.) needed for the maintenance of the body. A similar electromagnetic signal is sent to the heart so that it determines the frequency of its beats (this is why, in case of cardiac arrest, effort is made to provide again the trigger for the resumption of the heartbeat through an electric shock).

This information, coming to us through the planets which reflect the sunlight, is attracted by the core of the Earth, runs through our body and helps it absorb the elements needed in the geographic area where we reside. At the same time, essential nutritious elements are sent to the flora, the fauna and the water through the same radiation, so that the food chain of an area has continuity and each form is useful to the others.

In every geographical zone the flora, the fauna and the water contain specific elements that are shared with the inhabitants. These elements are necessary for the preservation of life in a particular zone; this is why the locals must nourish themselves on these elements. For example, the inhabitants in Central Africa need the elements in the vegetables, the fruit and the animals that live in that area. Because the water has "memory" and particular qualities – which will be analyzed in the next chapter – when we travel far from our country and consume the local water, it is possible to experience disturbance in our digestive system. The best solution is to drink bottled water, and if possible, of the same company.

If, for example, an body shows lack of some elements because of some pressure from thought, even if these elements are administered to him through a pharmaceutical treatment or with pills, they are not going to be absorbed by his body, because they will lack the planetary information that activates, through the pituitary gland, the intake and absorption of these particular elements.

These elements are present everywhere, in all foods. If the body functions well, it will find and absorb calcium even from the greens. But when it does not function properly, it cannot absorb calcium even from milk! The problem caused by repeated thoughts and fixations is located in the assimilation of the elements and not in their intake through the food. And absorption depends on the state of the body.

As repeated, often contradictory, thoughts accumulate in the mind, pressure is exerted in the brain. And, insofar as there is pressure in the brain, the pituitary gland finds it difficult to receive the information (particularly from the planets that are more remote) and hence to inform the neurotransmitters on the kind of nutritional elements the body needs. The result is that the person suffers from anemia, which is different for each type:

Type A has manganese fluctuations and iron deficiency*, problems in the function of the heart and brain sensitivity.

------

*Iron constitutes one of the essential elements of our nutrition and plays a decisive role in our body's intake of oxygen. This happens through a complicated process which, to a large extent, is due to its chemical properties. The human body contains approximately 75mg of iron per kilogram of mass, taking fat

Type B shows magnesium fluctuations linked to thrombophilia (heart condition), the nervous system, lack of vitamin D* and B12, and also to rheumatoid arthritis.

---

into account too. About three fourths of the total proportion of iron is found in the molecules of hemoglobin and myoglobin. The latter has a greater capacity of oxygen absorption and is a reservoir of oxygen for the body. It is not accidental that it is an ingredient of the heart and the skeleton. A large proportion of iron is also stored in the liver, the spleen, and the bones. Iron compounds are also responsible for the transportation of oxygen to the cells. That explains why iron deficiency, anemia caused by lack of iron, has symptoms of fatigue. This type of anemia is found almost exclusively in young people, as well as in women of reproductive age. Because iron is stored in our body, adult males rarely present anemia because of lack of iron. Typical sources of iron are spinach and liver.

*Vitamin D is the product of synthesis coming mainly from exposure to solar radiation. Very few foods contain vitamin D. The most important role of vitamin D is the increase in the absorption of calcium and sulfate from the intestine. Even if the nutrition is rich in calcium, without an adequate quantity of vitamin D, the calcium cannot be absorbed. Vitamin D also strengthens the immune system, and it may protect against some forms of cancer. Chronic lack of vitamin D may also increase the risk of rheumatoid arthritis, insulin resistance and other. The synthesis of vitamin D is facilitated by the consumption of foods of animal origin (especially liver, beef and eggs), dairy products (milk, cheese, and butter), some fish (sardines, herring, salmon and tuna) and pulses.

Type C presents copper fluctuations and deficiency in vitamin C*, which causes problems in the arteries (heart) and loosening of the joints.

The three types react differently to tension caused by a disordered function: in type A we observe panic in action, in type B anxiety towards the execution of action and in type C pain and sorrow.

Detoxifying diet

Quite often, I stress the need to have a balanced diet. I have compiled a detox diet that needs to be followed for three or four weeks or, in serious cases, until health is restored. This diet does not deprive the body of any nutritious substances. It does not allow acidic foods, yeast or leaven, because they are highly

---

*(Vitamin C is water-soluble. It is essential for certain metabolic functions of the body, like the synthesis of collagen, the stability of the blood vessels, the metabolism of aminoacids and the release of hormones in the epinephrids. The daily needs of the human body in vitamin C are great and reach 70-80 mg. It is found in citrus fruit (oranges, lemons, tangerines, etc.), in tomatoes and in fresh vegetables. It is essential for the resistance of the body against the common cold and for strong gums.

acidic. Of course, this is determined by the type of illness and our physician's advice. However, we should avoid the foods this diet does not allow.

When in pressure, the body does not function in a balanced way, and, as mentioned already, each human type tends to store the calcium oxalate in different areas. Type A stores it in the skin and the surface of the organs, and consequently suffers from xerodermia and cirrhosis of the liver. Type B stores it in the joints and suffers from ankylosing spondylitis or crystallization in the joints, resulting in their severe deterioration (rheumatoid arthritis). Type C stores it in the blood, and suffers from arteriosclerosis. The arteries calcify and marked symptoms occur on the visible capillary vessels (small red lines).

In the following pages, I am putting forth the detox diet, as well as some directions on how to bake no yeast bread and make yeast-free cheese.

In addition, I particularly recommend to people with problems in their digestive system or those who suffer from constipation to avoid roasted nuts and prefer raw nuts. I advise those suffering from spastic colitis to avoid pulses as a main course (they certainly need pulses, and they should have them in small quantities, accompanying their meal)., I recommend to those suffering from ulcerative colitis to avoid all nuts. I also advise type A people to avoid drinking, because they have a tendency to create cirrhosis of the liver (psychogenic). The same advice applies to all B types, who have high systolic pressure.

If an acidic substance happens to come to contact with an area where we have a wound, we will experience acute stinging pain. The same applies to our internal organs. When there are inflammations in our gastrointestinal system (particularly in the esophagus) caused by high disorder, we should not burden our body with acidic food, because it will cause spasticity and pain.

How dangerous is lemon, when there is high disorder, is confirmed by the fact that even seeing someone eating a lemon automatically makes our body to secrete excessive amounts of saliva in order to neutralize the poison and protect us from gastric problems.

Nutrition is the key not only to weight control, but also to the total health and well-being. Besides, it has the power to rebalance our body the chemistry.

When a body is at a state of balance, it suffers no complaints and no restrictions in the diet are necessary.

Detox Diet

Recommended for three weeks or, in case of high disorder, for as long as it is deemed necessary for the disorder to return to normal levels. In general, it is not allowed to have acidic food, yeast and whatever comes from fermentation.

Not allowed

Cheese (feta, kasseri, yellow cheese)
Yogurt
Bread with yeast or/and leaven.
Sour fruit (unripe)
Tomatoes
Lemon
Vinegar
Ketchup/mustard
Pickled or bitter olives
Pickles
Beer/wine/champagne (in general, beverages that come from fermentation).
Whatever other you feel causes heartburn
Lunch and dinner must not be the same, because, if one eats small quantities from the same food noon and evening, it works as a weight loss diet.

In cases of <u>cancer</u>, apart from the above foods, it is not allowed to eat sugar and dairy products.

Allowed

Cream cheese (manouri), soft cheese, mozzarella and all fresh creamy cheeses.
Feta cheese, produced with the method recommended below.
Milk
Fresh cream (healing for the gastrointestinal system).
Unleavened bread (recipes follow)
Sweet, ripe fruit (apples, pears, merlin oranges, etc.)
Pasta
Rice (not pilaf)
Potatoes
Olives sweet 'throumbes' (prepared without vinegar or lemon)
Fat-free meat
Fish
Beverages produced through distillation (ouzo, tsipouro, whiskey, cognac etc.) in small quantities, except if the disease does not allow them

It is also allowed to have all foods not listed in the list on the left

Quantities must be small and there should be variety in each meal.

BREAD WITHOUT YEAST

1st Recipe

- ½ kilo (1 lb) of flower (any kind or a combination of 2-3 kinds)
- 1 teaspoon of baking powder
- 1 teaspoon of salt
- ½ teaspoon of sugar or honey (optional) – the honey should be diluted in some lukewarm water
- 1 teacup of oil
- 1 packet of soda (bicarbonate)

Lukewarm water, enough to make dough soft. Optionally, some sesame seeds to dash over. Mix the ingredients and knead for a while. Bake in preheated oven at 400o F for 45 minutes.

2nd Recipe

- ½ kilo (1 lb) of flour (any kind or a combination of 2-3 kinds)
- ½ or 1 teaspoon of baking powder
- 1 teaspoon of sugar or honey (optional) – the honey should be diluted in some lukewarm water
- 1 heaped spoonful of cooking butter, margarine or any other butter you prefer

- Lukewarm water, enough to make dough soft
- Optionally, some sesame seeds to dash over

Rub the flour and butter together until the mixture resembles breadcrumbs. Add the rest of the ingredients and knead for a while. Bake in preheated oven at 400o F for 45 minutes.

FETA TYPE CHEESE (NOT FERMENTED)

- 1 litre fresh milk
- ½ kilo of fresh sour soft cheese (mizethra)
- salt

Mash the cheese using a fork. Moisten a pan and pour the milk in. Heat the milk in high temperature and stir continuously with a wooden spoon. When the milk boils, remove it from he heat. Add the cheese and as much salt as you like. Bring to a low fire to boil slowly. The cheese will curdle and come to the surface. Line a colander with a cheese cloth or muslin. Slowly pour the curdled milk into the colander. Squeeze and leave it to strain for two to ten hours, depending on how hard you want it to be. The water remaining in the saucepan can be used as brine to preserve the cheese.

HEALTH RESTORATION

I can emit energy from my hands in the form of a photon beam (bio-photons) which I can 'see' and direct to the suffering points of the body. Sometimes this luminous energy acts as an electrical beam, destroying the sick tissue. Other times the energy acts as magnetic beam, removing the sick tissue and directing it to the disposing channels of the body.

This electromagnetic treatment lowers the hormonal disorder, helping the body return to its normal function. It is sent directly to the problem.

By talking and explaining to people, I try to touch their soul in order to help them make new decisions, detach themselves from the problems and bring the best possible balance in their lives. And all this, by embracing them with love.

I particularly insist that **we must understand that the difficulty does not lie in learning new ways to**

lead our lives, but in un-learning, undoing the old ways that lead us to dead ends and increase our disorder.

It sometimes happens that people come hastily, only to take and go, without giving themselves the chance to feel the joy of change, and a smile to me. This makes me sad, because I feel that these people came to me like simple consumers who went to buy their groceries. They are in a hurry to return where their problem was created and they do not stay to get the answer of how this problem began in order to avoid it the next time. This attitude is what hurts me more than anything else.

The energizing of water

Apart from the electromagnetic help I offer to people that come to me, I also energize water, so that they can drink it and help their body even further. I would like, at this point, to give some brief information regarding the power of water, before I proceed to specific incidents.

Water is one of the three basic ingredients of our

material world. Our planet at the initial stages of its creation was entirely covered with water. In adult people 75% of their body is made up of water, and the percentage is higher in infants. It is the main element that can carry every genetic/energy information stored in its molecules and atoms.

Many experiments have shown that water is intelligent, it possesses intelligence – and how could this not be so, when it partakes to the Absolute Intelligence of the Universal World.

Once I was visited by someone who suffered from liver cancer. After receiving the treatment, the results were impressive. His doctor, a lady that was supervisor of the haematological department of a hospital, telephoned me and asked if she could visit me. She wanted to bring with her two patients who suffered from thalassemia and one from cancer. The meeting took place, and after my intervention, they gave me two bottles of water to energize it, so they could use it for an experiment.

A month later, the doctor came with the findings of the experiment with the energized water, which she had the idea to try it out in the following way: she chose ten patients with thalassemia and one with cancer, five men and five women, having an average

age of thirty five years. After the first blood tests, she gave each patient a glass of energized water to drink – the patients did not know that it was energized – and asked them to repeat the blood tests in an hour.

The results of the tests thrilled her, because, within just an hour, and only with a little water, the cancer indices CEA, CA 15-3, CA 19-9, CA 125, the indices for liver function and the atherosclerotic indices all showed clear improvement.

On Monday 1st April 2007, the neurologist doctor Dimitris Zaglis visited me holding an infrared camera. The purpose was to photograph the energizing of water. I shall here describe the obvious changes that all those present could detect with their own eyes in the images. There were also other changes, in the molecular structure of the water.

The doctor took a photograph of the first bottle of water. In the photo with the infrared camera one can see that the water in the interior of the bottle has a light green color. I passed my hands once or twice over the bottle without touching it. The water was energized. The bottle was photographed again. The color of the water was now blue.

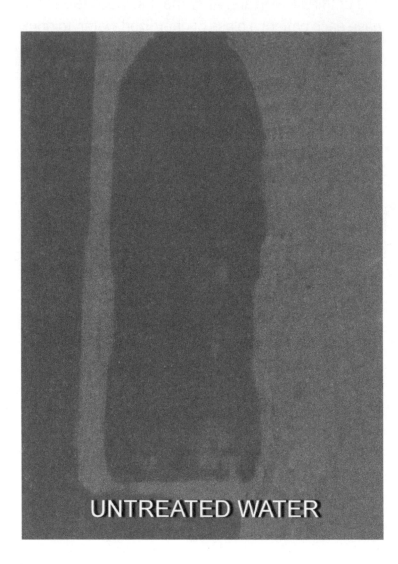

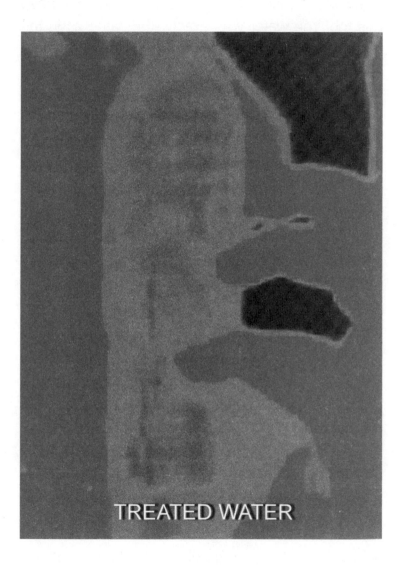

We took a second bottle and the doctor photographed this too. The water was exactly the same as in the previous bottle before the energizing; it had a light green color. I proceeded to energize it for cancer. In just a few the seconds the water turned into a dark blue color and one could see scatterd red spots in it.

The energy intervention and its imaging

Of course, in some cases the results – because of the particularities of certain diseases – are so obvious that there can be no doubt. In other cases, one needs a diagnosis to confirm the results through orthodox medical methods.

This is when the EEA method (Energy Emission Analysis) or, otherwise, ETD (Emergetische Terminalpunkt Diagnose) came to our assistance. This method was developed by Dr Peter Mandel in Germany, in the '70s.

The EEA method (Energy Emission Analysis)

In August 2007, a study was published examining

the possibility of distance interaction in the human bioenergy field. In other words, the particular way in which the radiation and the phenomenology in the photos changed before and after the influence of the therapist, who in this case was George Paschalidis.

The study was carried out by Christos Colettas using equipment 'ETD Acron 2000', in accordance with the Kirlian-EEA analysis. The data and the images that follow are included in Christos Colettas' study.

All cases were treated in long distance. In fact, from the distance of 300 km. There was no visual or tactile contact, only by telephone for the necessary communication. There was no previous acquaintance with George Paschalidis, neither was he given any information on the subjects. The survey lasted from November 2005 to September 2006, and every participant was examined separately.

Seventeen people were examined in total. The process was the same as always, when the participants are next to the therapist. First an 'analysis', i.e. a 'diagnosis' of the state of the participant took place, and then the therapist intervened.

Before and after the intervention of the therapist, a Kirlian image of the subjects was taken in order to compare data regarding the subjects' state with data of the therapist examining subjects.

The method uses the imprint of the bioenergy field or aura from the fingertips of the hands and feet known as "Kirlian image". It has taken its name from the name of the Russian electrician, engineer and academic Semyon Kirlian who invented it. The imprinted image bears a lot of information. It depicts the energy flow of the functions and dysfunctions that take place in the human body.

Energy meridians end in the fingertips and the analysis of the emitted radiation from the fingertips makes is possible to arrive at safe conclusions regarding the total state of the body on the dynamic (energy) level, even at an early and asymptomatic stage.

The method that analyzes the images

As a first step to the understanding Kirlian image analysis with the help of EEA, it must be stated that the flow from all extremes must show, in the ideal situation, a specific harmony. The subject must radiate, with equal intensity, an energy flow neither too dense nor too sparse and various features that suggest the existence of a disorder should be absent.

These include:

Reduced or totally absent radiation from the whole hand, foot or a finger, or even from a segment of the finger.

Absence of the flow or particularly dense charge at isolated segments or accumulation of particular round stigmata on them.

The shape of the flow in each finger (round or oval) must be clearly visible on each finger.

Naturally, there are plenty of details that have to be taken into account, yet in the pictures that follow those points are marked, so that they can be easily comprehended by the non-specialist in the analysis of such pictures..

The letters X and V were used, where X indicates disorder, while V indicates restoration or partial restoration of the problem (ability to reverse the problem.)

In most cases those problems are not discussed on the pictures, but are left to the reader to notice. Sometimes arrows are used, to point to the problematic sections.

Indicatively, we present Kirlian images of five participants:

CASE STUDY 1

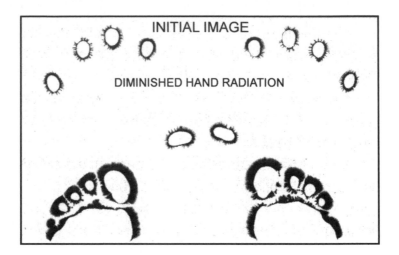

INITIAL IMAGE

DIMINISHED HAND RADIATION

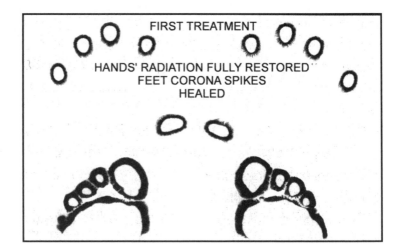

FIRST TREATMENT

HANDS' RADIATION FULLY RESTORED
FEET CORONA SPIKES
HEALED

CASE STUDY 9

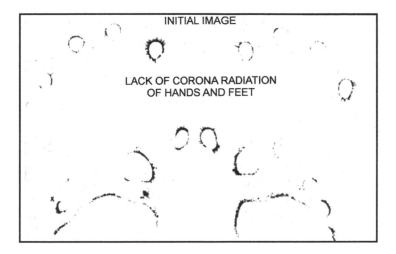

INITIAL IMAGE

LACK OF CORONA RADIATION
OF HANDS AND FEET

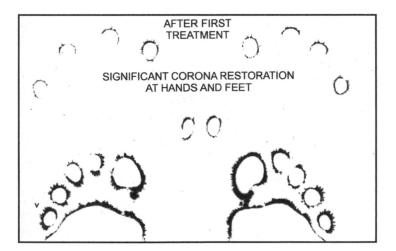

AFTER FIRST
TREATMENT

SIGNIFICANT CORONA RESTORATION
AT HANDS AND FEET

CASE STUDY 9 (CONTINUED)

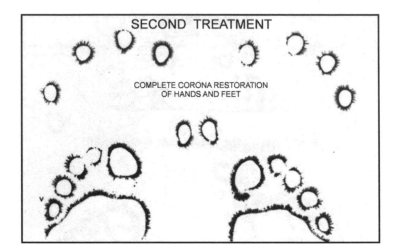

SECOND TREATMENT

COMPLETE CORONA RESTORATION
OF HANDS AND FEET

CASE STUDY 10

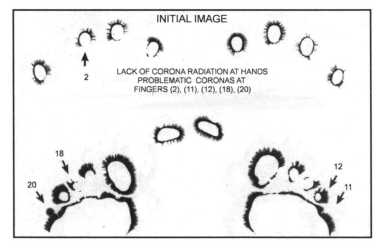

INITIAL IMAGE

LACK OF CORONA RADIATION AT HANDS
PROBLEMATIC CORONAS AT
FINGERS (2), (11), (12), (18), (20)

CASE STUDY 10 (CONTINUED)

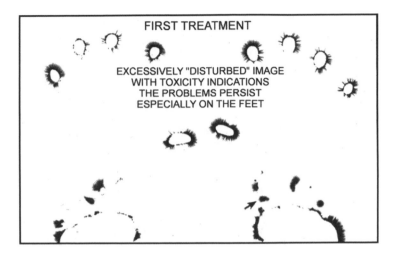

FIRST TREATMENT

EXCESSIVELY "DISTURBED" IMAGE
WITH TOXICITY INDICATIONS
THE PROBLEMS PERSIST
ESPECIALLY ON THE FEET

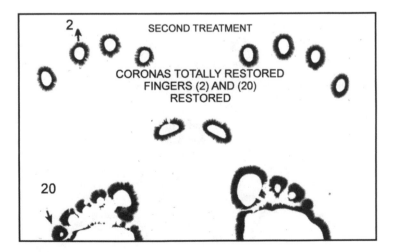

SECOND TREATMENT

CORONAS TOTALLY RESTORED
FINGERS (2) AND (20)
RESTORED

CASE STUDY 10 (CONTINUED)

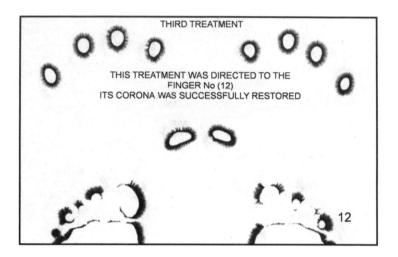

CASE STUDY 15

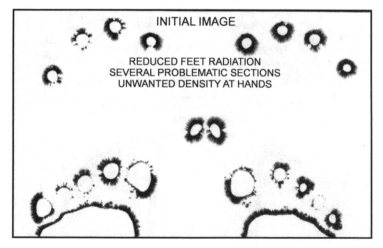

CASE STUDY 15 (CONTINUED)

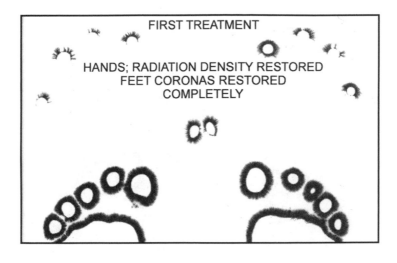

FIRST TREATMENT

HANDS; RADIATION DENSITY RESTORED
FEET CORONAS RESTORED
COMPLETELY

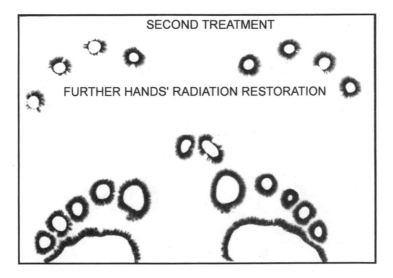

SECOND TREATMENT

FURTHER HANDS' RADIATION RESTORATION

CASE STUDY 16

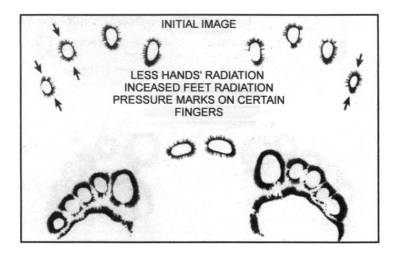

INITIAL IMAGE

LESS HANDS' RADIATION
INCEASED FEET RADIATION
PRESSURE MARKS ON CERTAIN
FINGERS

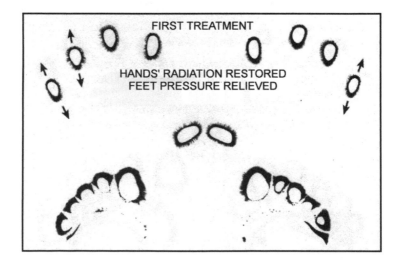

FIRST TREATMENT

HANDS' RADIATION RESTORED
FEET PRESSURE RELIEVED

SURVEY CONCLUSION:

A clear and often catalytic influence was observed by the therapist's intervention on those subjected to examination, an influence that cannot be attributed to the 'luck' factor or the normal fluctuations of the energy flow.

SEGMENTAL ANALYSIS
Of a body though measuring its conductance before and after energy therapy

The neurologist Dimitris Zaglis used the system IMEDIS EXPERT for the segmental record of the conductance and its correlation to the function of the autonomous nervous system and the internal organs.

The measuring took place on May 11, 2008 and 14 people took part in it on a voluntary basis, selected among the patients waiting to see George Paschalidis. The infrared camera Guide IRIM3 was used.

Three pairs or electrodes were placed on the soles, the palms and the forehead. Each person was measured before and after the therapeutic intervention. During therapy the patient was not touched and the hand of the therapist approached the body from a distance of approximately five centimeters (the closest), to one or two meters (the furthest away). With four of the patients, the therapeutic intervention was performed from a distance, with the therapist being in a separate room and at a distance of seven meters at least.

In each case, the therapeutic intervention caused quick or immediate changes in skin conductance as a result of the change of the state of the autonomous nervous system. This implies a change of functionality not only of the skin, but also of the internal organs. The images show an immediate and visible difference (the images are in the next two pages).

It is important to mention that these changes are achieved in times that range approximately within a minute. The simultaneous recording of conductance at the time of therapy depicts a change of conductance in times measuring in seconds.

To conclude, George Paschalidis' intervention causes a change in the function of the autonomous nervous system in a very short time. It also definitively proves that it can change the function of the internal organs.

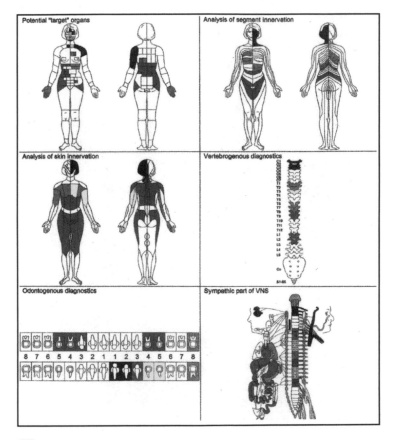

Sharply expressed hyperfunction
Expressed hyperfunction
Moderately expr. hyperfunction
Weakly expressed hyperfunction
Norm
Weakly expressed hypofunction
Moderately expr. hypofunction
Expressed hypofunction
Sharply expressed hypofunction

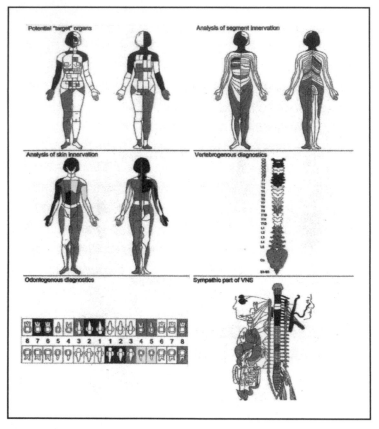

Sharply expressed hyperfunction
Expressed hyperfunction
Moderately expr. hyperfunction
Weakly expressed hyperfunction
Norm
Weakly expressed hypofunction
Moderately expr. hypofunction
Expressed hypofunction
Sharply expressed hypofunction

With the use of an infrared camera we also took photos of a patient with periarthritis in the right shoulder.

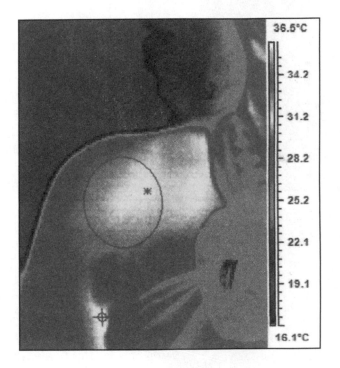

*The area depicted in yellow,
indicates the affected area.*

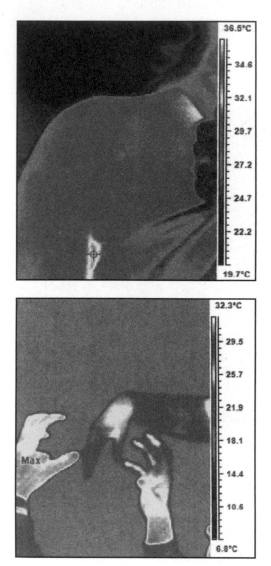

After the treatment the suffering area of the patient appears in green colour, which indicates pain relief, as the patient also mentioned.

In the third picture we see the hands of the healer guiding the "yellow" – which indicates the affected area – to the patient's wrist, which then will be eliminated from the patient's body.

Today the first cycle of research has been completed in a public hospital in Athens, with 60 volunteers, 20 of each type. The sample is small, but soon we will continue with more volunteers. In the near future, we shall be able to identify our type with the use of a simple X-ray, and do so, not only in order to ascertain our dominant psychological characteristics, but also in order to be in a position to heal our body at the proper time.

CONCLUSION

We know, from our readings, that the thoughts and the words that produce these thoughts have tremendous power. We believed that this was just another theory. Following George Paschalidis' advice we realized, here, at the end of his book, that thoughts and words may also lead us astray, make us lose our target, because they have the power to attune the frequency of our cells to the frequency of good, health, joy, harmony and love.

People who think and act evil, are, of course only few. Most of us only have de-formed, vague thoughts. The Universe, however, has a shape, has a form, is shapely, beautiful, does not make room for ugliness and indefiniteness.

George Paschalidis himself remarks on this:

"When one agrees with something indefinite, one offends God in oneself. Search for the words. What

each word means. Do not express yourselves and do not think in indefinite concepts. Be careful with the words you use."

He also says:

'We thought that there are two ways; one of the good and one of evil. Yet, there is a third way, that of doubt. Few are those who follow the way of the evil. Most of you follow the road of doubt; the worm enters easily in you. In this way, however, you are not on the road of the good. Cast doubt away from you"

And then he advises us:

"Smile. This is the first expression of love. A smile can open up the pituitary gland and facilitate the flow of information to the body. And a body that is full with good information has no room for disease. When you hear good information or a word of truth, this is acknowledged in the genetic root and you change in a second. Change is but a 'click', it can erase of the past. You will then see that you can actually smile and draw energy from the right source. Smile, learn how to live and enjoy life".

George, always with a smile in his face, when asked who he is, always comes with the disarming reply: "I am just George".

Polychronis, friend of George Paschalidis, in a

stanza of his poem 'This is how the poet saw me', dedicated to him in 2008, writes:

I am but nothing.
a silent brook
that joined the sea of faith,
and serenely sails.
I offer love and joy
and ask nothing in return.

The name George comes from 'γεωργός' (georgos) that signifies the farmer, the person that cultivates the land. George Paschalidis indeed was a farmer tilling the land, but since 2002 he "changed crops". He cultivates souls of people that are the key to our health.

We should not make the mistake to identify him as a therapist (he himself does not like this term and only uses it as a convention). For, his goal is to cultivate the seed of love that we all carry in our genetic luggage. In the Foreword we had expressed the wish that science benefit from George Paschalidis' Knowledge, so that in turn it will manage to expand its service to man.

"Your work takes place in the domain of the Visible, the Manifested. Let us work together", he tells the scientists.

A happy coincidence gave George Paschalidis access to the Invisible Morphogenetic Field (that stores all information on life and man) and he offers himself, humbly, to share with medicine all that he 'sees' through the 'window' opened to him, so that this 'know-how' is spread for the benefit of all of us.

This is a message of hope for humanity.

Let us listen to him.

OPENING OF LOVE

Which poetic words could touch us more than love itself?

Love and life are not words, but actions.

"We should open our hearts, because we all have love deep inside, in some remote obscure corner, tucked away and frozen beneath our thoughts and our musts".

Without words, without conditions, love becomes a warm wind that unlocks our frozen hearts and makes them quiver. Then the eyes of our souls take a glimpse of the beauty around us and all seem delightful and fine.

How else could you so generously become one with the people? To give is love and life. It is when you see your fellow being as your brother; it is only then that you discover the crystal laughter in your soul then the beauty of life emerges free from all doubt and guilt.

"God has placed us in a Heaven. Enjoy it. It is a sin not to enjoy it. Love, love yourselves first, in order to be able to love others!"

Boundless love opens in front of us the true path for our lives. An opening of Love, giving us answers to all our queries for a substantial, joyful and full passage from this life.

And then everything is love and joy, from hugging what warms a cold heart to singling and dancing to our favorite melody.

Love is always a torrent, sweeping us to happiness. Love means *"I cease to be me, and become you"*.

It is only then that the beauty and joy of life open their arms to us and their melody leads us to endless happiness.

Yet, how many of us have this feeling of love alive in their hearts? For how many of us *"Love is patient, love is kind and is not jealous; love does not brag and is not arrogant, does not act unbecomingly; it does not seek its own, is not provoked, does not take into account a wrong suffered, does not rejoice in unrighteousness, but rejoices with the truth; bears all things, believes all things, hopes all things, endures all things. Love never fails."?*

Who can happily and with a jubilant soul say that we have love? No one, no one. No one can convey these emotions to such extent".

We meet various people every day. It is difficult to make them our friends and very rare for them to be true friends.

But is not impossible to be humane.

PATH OF LIFE

People are innocent. Guilty is he who has made science an inconceivable deception. He who deceives people, drawing them to his own 'beliefs'.

Most times, people argue with God, ignoring that HE will never abolish freedom. He gave man the right to choose, learn and revise, because God wants people to be his children, not his robots.

The establishment is tough, and the flesh has a tight grip on its passions. It does not separate itself from them. True war and struggle are within us. Only God's spirit change us. Every other possibility was explored and failed. In the beginning they appeared to be producing some work that in the process was cancelled. Only Love can lead man to Deification that is the oxygen of Eternal Life.

If people believed in the love of God, with a vivid faith, the Kingdom of heaven would have been established here on Earth.

APPENDIX

Testimonials

On 06.06.2005, I decided to ask those who would wish to write a testimonial for the experience of their visit. Here, I put before you some of the hundreds of these testimonials:

24.6.2009
Aristotle said that our father gives us life, but the teacher gives us good life. This is precisely what George Paschalidis gave me, becoming, in the few meetings we had, and without him realizing it, the best teacher I ever had. This first time I heard him, and despite the fact that some of the truths he was telling people were already heard, I was reserved and doubtful. I had heard that George cures, but I could not understand that the discussion I had with him

was helping towards the therapy. Some 2-3 hours later I was so anxious, I just wanted to receive his therapy so that I could get up and go.

Fortunately, I now know how important it is to know how to listen. And when I say 'listen' I mean to really listen to the other, without trying to falsify or interrupt him to just how little we know. To my view, the only way to improve our lives is to have the guts to acknowledge that a lot of what we already know is sketchy or entirely false and, further, to have the courage to erase the old beliefs and adopt the new ones. To do all this, however, we must be humble, because only by controlling our old Ego are we able to learn anew.

Thus, George, with very simple words, helped me go beyond the misery, superstition, guilt, egotism, jealousy and other destructive feelings and preconceptions that have been tormenting me for years. He also helped me understand my nature and my natural inclination towards certain behaviors, drawing from the taxonomy of types. Here, I would like to refer to what George says on 'fixation'. Never before had someone explained to me the nature of fixation and how negatively it affects us. I now know that fixation not only makes us sick, but also keeps us imprisoned in the worst jail – one that we ourselves have built for ourselves.

❦

X. had lost her vision since 3.3.2003. Until today that we came to George, she was living in darkness. Now she has started to see colors, shapes and, bit by bit, even figures. Have you ever imagined your life without colors? Do you know what it is like to have darkness as your only company, day and night, through all seasons? Only then will you understand her condition. Until today, she has not yet seen her niece, aged a year and a half. But as from today, she will start seeing her!

I had serious back problems for years; I was in pain; I couldn't lift anything, not even my bag. Today, I bent for the first time with no pain at all. I am flying out of happiness!

From the depths of my heart, all happiness to you, George!

❦

I am F. I was advised to come; I had no idea what this was all about. I came to George with a health problem. My right arm was ankylosed in the elbow. He loosened the stiffness; he opened up the ankylosis without me feeling a thing!

May God bless you, George to perform your miracles.

Thank you, F.B.

✑

Today, 26.6.08 Mr. George helped me. I could not hear from the left ear, but now I began hearing very well.

I thank him very much.

✑

My name is T.L. I was born deaf and mute, but now my hearing is gradually being restored.

I pray to God, and wish you well, so that you will go on offering your services to people. T.L.

✑

19.6.2005

I am S. Ten years ago I saw my skin covered with a strange crust. I was scared. The doctors could not clean up my body from this bark. One day a telephone call changed my life. It was Easter 2003 when I was first told about George. I came with my parents. George told me, with a smile on his face, that in three weeks I would be clear. I told him that the doctors had told me to learn to live in this condition. George insisted 'You will be healed". It is now a year and a half since then. I am totally clean, I dress as I like, and I live as I like. I am happy, and I owe this to George.

I adore him and I thank him. S.

❧

My name is M. and I am one of the greatest skeptics. I always said that I need to see a miracle in order to believe. When I met George, I asked for his help in order to reduce my cholesterol that had reached to 380-400. No medication and no diet had any results and this was the reason I had a heart operation. A few days before I went on holidays I had some tests and I show that my cholesterol level had reached 380. I came to George and I asked him to help me. When I came back from my holidays, my cholesterol had dropped to 238. I never had such good results.

Thank you George.

❧

I had lost my voice for 4 months and I came to George. My voice came back as good as before. For me George is my second father. K.

❧

9.9.2006
This is our first visit to this wonderful man, who has the soul of a small child. This is my first experience. I had a problem with my right eye; my optical nerve was necrosed. He cured it completely.

A sincere thank you, which is something very small.

X.Z.

September 2006
My name is N. I had been trying for three years to become pregnant but without success. I underwent two operations, had three lumbar punctures and five IVFs, all to no avail. I felt bitterly disappointed. One day a friend of mine told me about George. I felt that I had just received a message of optimism. I contacted him immediately and from the first minute he gained my confidence. I am now on my 4th month pregnant, full of love and in very good mood.

I pray to God to keeps George well and that with His help to give health and happiness to the whole world. N.K.

26.9.2006

I had a problem with my knee. I was suffering from acute pains, I could not work, walk or run. I am 28 years old. Now I am in no pain at all, and the liquid from my knee is completely gone.

I pray to God that He keeps you well. I thank you with all my heart. N.L.

18.7.2008

Obstetric paralysis... Since I was a young child I never stopped going to doctors, but without results.. Today, at the age of 47, having known George, I finally had some positive results. I was so happy when I saw my arm raised like all normal people.

I thank you George and may God keep you well. So that you keeps us well too. Thank you. M.

12.2.2006

I came to George having been told by friends that they had been cured by him. I came for my right ear that could not hear since I was 18. The doctors had diagnosed that the verve of hearing was necrosed and so they could do nothing about it.

And yet Mr. George cured my ear and now I can

hear perfectly. This happened on my first visit. At the same time he helped my arm that was suffering from tendonitis in the elbow, deep in the bone.

Thank you very much Mr. George. I wish you are always well and strong and be of help to all those that have health problems. E.L.

∽✕∾

7.10.2008

For 15 years I had been suffring from myopic astigmatism with keratoconus and recently I developed atrial fibrillation. In less than three minutes my vision improved dramatically, and from 0.5/10 that was the level of my vision, I saw almost to 5/10 while the blur in my vision was almost gone! It is noteworthy that a top ophthalmologist in England had told me that only a transplant could help me, but with the chances for success evenly balanced.

Words are not enough to thank you. K.S.

∽✕∾

3.9.2008

On 21.7.2008, an accident took place and as a result the motorcyclist suffer fracture in seven ribs and lung puncture. His life was at risk in the first 24 hours. Mr. George was in a position to cure him from a distance and he left the hospital within a week. The doctors did not believe it! M.L.

✧

1.4.2006
I had extra-systolic arrhythmia and I was in pain. I came to Mr. George and he cured me. I had tests and they showed I was all right. I thank Mr. George .

✧

1.4.2006
I thank God and Mr. George for the help he gave me along with the help of God concerning a serious health problem I had. I came here with two crutches and pain on the leg, and left holding only one crutch and feeling much better. Thank you. K.M.

✧

1.3.2006
I came to Mr. George for a problem my daughter had. While I was sitting, I heard that he had cured a blind person. I then had the desire to use his help, because since birth I could only see from one eye. In ten minutes he helped me see from both eyes.
I can't thank him enough. M.X.

✧

20.10.2005

Since 31 August 2005, I lost my sight in my right eye. I was hospitalized. I was told by the doctors that I was suffering from a rare syndrome, and there was no therapy for me in the entire world. But I learned about you, Mr. George, and I came and found you. In less than a quarter of an hour, I regained my sight. A hundred per cent (100%) vision. Proved. After this I went to the doctors who confirmed my vision in writing. The ophthalmologists could not believe what had happened. They called it a miracle. God bless you, George. E.

❧

19.1.2006

Since I was 10 years old I had a problem with my left ear. I had it till recently; I'm now 63 years old. George made me hear again within 5 minutes. I could hear again! Thank you so much, George, for what you did for me.

❧

29.3.2006

I heard about George and I decided to visit him. I have a problem with my ears and my waist. I finally visited George Paschalidis and I felt wonderfully. The blurred vision is gone. I do not need glasses to see far. My waist is better now, the pains have gone. I sincerely thank him. E.K.

≈

22.6.2006

My brother S. was in hospital for a month with sepsis. It took only a phone call to George and after three days my brother was literally flying! He came out of the intensive care unit and was saved. The doctors had told us that he was going to die. As for me, I had problems with my back, with pains and all, and after only one visit to George Paschalidis, the pains have gone. I thank him so much.

≈

I thank George Paschalidis. I was suffering with chondropathy of the knee (Chondromalacia patellae) and I could not walk properly; I was bedridden for two months. This, until my father met with George Paschalidis and brought me to him. After the third visit I was normal again! Normal walking and running! God bless you, George! M.G.

≈

26.2.2006

A week before coming to George my mother had been diagnosed with breast tumor. The doctors had decided to operate on her. Three days before she made the decision to come to Mr. George and after 15 minutes there was no tumor at all! We thank you so much!!! I wish you the best!!!

⤜⤛

Today, Wednesday 12 noon, I had my own experience. I had a problem in the chest, I had been to the doctors, and they told me I had a fibro adenoma (carcinoma) on the breast. They advised me to be operated on as soon as possible because it was getting bigger. Thus, after making the big decision we came to George and he made it disappear. I thank him from the bottom of my heart. D.K.

⤜⤛

I cannot believe what is happening to me. Two months ago I had horrible pains on my knee. I went to the doctor and had a magnetic tomography and I was diagnosed with meniscus tear. He gave me medicine and told me that if they do not cure me, I should undergo operation, because it was growing worse. Today, however, Wednesday 4.1.2006 I came to visit George. Until now I could not move my leg, and my knee was in pain. Now I can bend it with no pain at all. Thank you. H.G.

19.5.2005

How shall I start writing? When:

You have cured my wife who was suffering from breast cancer.

You have cured my niece who was suffering from colon cancer.

You have cured my sister in law who was suffering from cervical cancer.

You have cured my father who was suffering from colon cancer and dozens of other diseases that I had direct experience of in your place.

You are my father, my brother, my friend.

16.9.2006

I visited Mr. George in May 2006. I was suffering from multiple sclerosis, and at that time I was having a relapse, and all my body was numb. I was on cortisone and in a few days, I would start being on interferon (injections therapy for my entire life). The therapy never started as Mr. George removed the lesions from the brain and the neck, the numbness is gone and I am entirely well. Thank you very much.

With my love, S.L.

My name is M. I was preparing to go to hospital for a third time with a meniscus tear. What can I say? It is as if all pain disappeared into thin air.

∽⤬∽

Dear friend George, I heard once people talking about you in a clinic. I was waiting almost a year to be able to meet you. I have visited you five times, and today I feel wonderful and so healthy. So severe a problem, with my neck, my legs, my hands and now I am absolutely well. The cervical polyps and the polyps in my throat have completely disappeared and it was confirmed when I made a visit to my doctor and while I was preparing to undergo another operation to have them removed. I thank you from the bottom of my heart.

∽⤬∽

1.10.2006
After 20 years of suffering and after 20 years of being tormented, I so happened to visit George in order to have my child seen. My child, L. was going from good to better, a lot better, until one day he got up and walked. A very big thank you to George but, above all, to God.

∽⤬∽

My name is P. For two months my arm was in pain and I could not move it. I came to Mr. George and within ten minutes he cured me. He also cured my mother, who could not walk and suffered with pains in her legs. Now she gets up from the chair and walks without cramps and without pains! We thank you Mr. George

My mother had hurt her leg, and yet, after visiting George we left walking normally, while her neck felt absolutely normal, without the pain she was suffering from. My father also feels well from the waist up. Thank you very much. O.

I had this pain for 10 years. I went everywhere and I came here and you cured me. Thank you. L.

30.1.2007
When I contacted George for the first time on the phone, my wife was in surgery undergoing an operation for breast cancer. The subsequent tests proved normal. May God keep him well.

8.10.2006

I used to have psoriasis. I took medicine of ointments. Nothing. Three years ago miss out on my period. The doctor told me entering menopause. I came to Mr. George my friends told him about me. The next mo my pimples were gone and the color of my sk normal. My period, that had stopped, came ba the third day after my visit to George. I thank you much. S.

❧

I am suffering from scleroderma with visceral involvement. My disease is incurable;; there is only symptomatic treatment with cortisone and various medicines. I have been coming to George since February 2006 and I see a gradual diminishing of my swelling, I have higher endurance and I am not out of breath when speaking. Pulmonary hypertension is decreased to 8.5 units and I have stopped taking most of the medicine I used to take. I am breathing better and I have no breathlessness. I am gradually getting better. God bless you Mr. George. S.

❧

I had nodules on the thyroid and a slipped disc. I heard about George from my mother who had a scar in her retina, problems with her waist and her knees. After the therapy, the nodules were gone, I have no pains at all in my waist and the scar in my mother's eye has healed. I do thank you from the bottom of my heart, Mr. George!

❧

26.9.2006
When I came here I was dizzy, my head ached, front and back, and my right hand was trembling. Following the discussion with Mr. George I began to calm down. My hand stopped trembling, its strength came back and there were no more headaches.

I thank you so much.
I had gone to so many doctors to find a cure for the pains I had in the waist, the hips and the legs. There was no cure, either with injections or with the medicine. I came to George and in ten minutes all the pain was gone. I thank him so much. D.K.

❧

I was suffering from lung cancer. I came to Mr. George and I was fully cured. God give him health to go on curing all the ailing people. And I thank God again that led me here to be healthy again. K.L.

❧

I came to George today, 10.9.2006. My right leg has osteoarthritis for 10 years. As a result I was suffering from friction of the joint; I could not bend the leg and I had to drag it. The pain was excruciating. Yet, due to George, 10 minutes ago I started walking properly.

❧

Since 11 years ago, my husband and I were trying to conceive a second child, but this proved impossible. We had been to many doctors, who told us there was nothing wrong, having done their tests and ultrasound scanning. A friend of ours, having seen our efforts and repeated tests to so many doctors, recommended that we see Mr. George. He received us gladly, and he told us: "Do not worry". Now, my baby is two months old. A thousand thanks. F.L.

❧

I had malignant tumor in the cyst. Every Wednesday I used to go to the hospital, and I suffered a lot with the injections treatment. Until the moment I came to Mr. George. I was fully cured. B.N.

❧

I had lung cancer and muscle failure. After the treatment all was restored to normal. This was confirmed by tests a couple of months later. K.O.

It was Holy Thursday when I visited Mr. George. A week before, the doctor had advised me to undergo a biopsy of the thyroid, to check whether I had cancer. At the same time I had suffered facial nerve paresis and I had persistent pains in the eye and the jaw. When leaving George I had no pain at all and also had this certainty that the biopsy will prove negative. Moreover, Mr. George told me that I had fiber adenoma in the chest and that he had touched something 'hard'. With the therapy, this point softened and the swelling disappeared. Th.L.

❧

A week before we came to George, my mother was diagnosed with tumor in the breast and it was decided to be operated on. Three days before the operation we came to Mr. George and 15 minutes later, the tumor did not exist. The whole family had come, and we were all shocked! My father suffers from ankylosing spondylitis, and with Mr. George's help, he felt great relief and relaxation. Also, my sister and I had other health problems that we did not want to tell him about and he found them one after the other and cured them! K.G.

❧

My mother had a tumor in the armpit, and was about to undergo an operation within a week. I met with George at a doctor's in Germany. Without even touching her, he eliminated her tumor. Th.E.

I was diagnosed with tumour in the liver. When I visited Mr. George, I heard him surprised to describe things about my health that nobody knew about, but also features of my character. I trusted him, and when I will have my next tests I am sure I will have nothing. E.P.

Mr. George's love is so true, so authentic, that it heals everything. For 15 years I had impaired hearing. Now I can hear and feel the low voices that I was missing from my life... E.L.

28.4.2006
He helped me and my family with the problems we had for years, within a few minutes. I regained my hearing by 100%, something the doctors had deemed impossible... N.K.

I came to meet Mr. George and stay with him for an afternoon. I stayed for 5 days, watching and experiencing his work for over fourteen hours a day... I saw how tirelessly he spreads his love and smile to all with no exception. To relieve people from pain, to heal, to listen to their problems, to understand them and advise them, to forgive them and not to get angry with them – Well, I did. I did get angry, I got enraged when some people would come with the hearts locked up in order to "demand' therapy, to "demand" to learn what Mr. George does and how he does it... And he, ever so patient, with peace and serenity.. K.

❧

28.3.2006
A thousand thanks to Mr. George who made me well from a polypus. When he saw me, he told me that in three weeks it will 'drop' by itself. So it did. I had tests and they showed I was clean. S.G.

❧

I was suffering from psoriasis. I was cured. What a relief! L.

❧

I was diagnosed with multiple sclerosis. After seven

months, all lesions have disappeared and so have my mobility problems.

❧

I had multiple sclerosis and aneurysm in the brain. I am walking. My problems are over! D.K.

❧

I had multiple sclerosis, pains and numbness. Everything is now gone, and my walking is restored.

❧

I brought my nephew to Mr. George, who suffered with multiple sclerosis. After the first therapy all the pains and the numbness were gone. After the second therapy, the MRI was not showing any lesions in the neck, and those in the brain were reduced.

❧

I had two loves in life to direct my energy: gymnastics and dance. One day I got up from the bed and had excruciating pains in my left leg. I said to myself that it would pass. It got worse. The MRI scan showed a herniated intervertebral disc. The doctor said that from now on I should learn to live with my problem, and that I should forget anything that would tire my spinal column, that had become a concrete pillar.

After only the second visit to George, I was able to bend my waist and after the third all pain was gone. I am grateful! K.D.

❧

I am suffering with pains in the waist, affecting the right hip and leg. For three years, I went form one doctor to the other and they all said that I shall be in pain from now on. Yet, I am only 40 years old, and I cannot accept that I should live the rest of my life in this condition. George started the therapy and I used to bend trying to find were the pains had gone! We burst into laughing. I thank you so much, my God! You took the pain away through this man! Keep him well to continue helping people in the pain and sorrow they are into. S.M.

❧

8 years ago I injured myself seriously in a football match. I did everything in the effort to find a cure. In vain. I came to Mr. George and now I am healed. G.L.

❧

My name is F. and I am a football player. On 24.12.05 I suffered a small injury on the left knee with a tear on the ligament, and I could not step on the foot. I was lucky, because I went to Mr. George and in less than 20 minutes the knee was working properly. Impressive, unprecedented!

❧

I was suffering with an acute pain in the arm and the shoulder; I had problems with the spinal column having undergone two operations on the 4th and 5th cervical vertebra. The entire left leg felt as if it wasn't there. It took only one visit for me to heal completely. I managed to sleep again. G.M.

❧

I was injured on the ribs with a fructure and I was suffering from acute pains. In five minutes my pains disappeared and so did the problem I had with my leg for 4 years; I could not step on it. A.A.

❧

I had a problem with my neck and the gastrointestinal system and now I am completely well. E.G.

❧

I was suffering from lateral epicondylitis on the right elbow, my arm was cramped and I needed an operation. I also had a problem with my waist, it needed an operation. George took off me all the burdens. P.K.

꙳

When I came the first time I was carried by others. I left here walking... no pain at all... I had tears of joy in my eyes... V.P.

꙳

I came here with pains and difficulties in walking. I am now walking perfectly; I couldn't even imagine I would one day be able to. R.L.

꙳

I had broken my arm; I was suffering for a year with the plaster cast. Three days before visiting Mr. George, the blades were removed from the wrist. I could not move it, I needed physiotherapy. In 5 minutes it was functioning as well as the left arm. He also cured my father, my brother and my mother. We all felt like human beings when we left! F.K.

꙳

I had pains on the carpal tunnels, high in the thighs, the neck, the shoulders and the back. It felt as if I was born again, no pains at all... A.P.

꙳

I had pains in the eye and the cyst. I am leaving my pains back in Alexandria. X.K.

I was suffering with my Postural Status. When I would get up I would faint. My therapy started on the phone, and then I came close. I thank you for the smile and the hospitality. I feel so grateful. E.L.

※

It is already a year since I came to see you. I was a graduate of Law School, and we came with my partner (and now husband) in order to show support to a friend who was suffering from multiple sclerosis and wanted to see you.

※

The moment you saw us and with no prior information from either me or anyone else, you immediately diagnosed that I was suffering from polycystic ovaries, a fact that would prove an obstacle in me having a baby. I was shocked how easy it was for you to have access to information only my doctor knew. Enchanted as I was and thrilled with all I was hearing about your miracles that were taking place those two days, I asked you to perform therapy on me concerning my ovarian problem.

Today, a year later, I have son who is three months

old. The doctors gave us as a possible conception date the day between 24 and 28 September 2006, the 4 days that followed my visit to you. I wish all the people that they open their heart to your blessing. I also hope that these tangible facts of healing do help people to abandon their skepticism and let healing take place... D.S.

❧

4.4.2006
It was ascertained medically that I had 5 nodules in the thyroid. When I came to George, he immediately told me so. He told me not to worry, and that in the next visit there will be only one nodule. So it came to be... S.R.

❧

In my first visit, after a difficult operation my disorder was 70%. On the third visit, the index had come down to 36%. I am all right! I thank everyone! Also, in the first visit I had a huge mole on my head that I was planning to have it removed. When I left, the mole fell in my hand. But all this is nothing compared to my son's case. He was suffering from acute pains, after a series of operations on the knee. There is no pain at all, now. He gathers strength and goes from good to better... I received a good lesson, LOVE CURES. Thank you. N.G.

After the first visit, I felt that things will go better from now on. Really, I feel I am alive again, in many aspects of my inner world. I suffered from depression, but now I have realized what I have hidden in me; powers that I was not in a position to see and understand... S.K.

∾

7.12.2005

I met with Mr. George during the most desperate time of my life. He told me on the phone what I was suffering from, before I told him. When I met him, he told me of other things as well, personal problems of my health and many other things that were tormenting me. One of the problems standing out was the operation I was about to have to remove stones from my gall bladder. Since my first visit, I was absolutely cured... B.K.

∾

Since 4 years he was suffering from polio. Legs so weak and walking with difficulty, the soles deformed. The doctors declared he would never walk, he does not move the legs when sitting. After receiving help from Mr. George he can lift the legs when he sits down and can now stretch them. T.K.

༄

I had stress, pressure in the head; I was seeing shadows and heard voices. I had interrupted my studies and was receiving medical treatment. Gradually, I stopped the medicine, I am well, and came back 7 months later to thank him... A.B.

༄

I thank God that brought you in my path at the right moment. I was suffering from advanced osteoarthritis in my left leg, a result of a chronic condition. I was born with a congenital exarthroma, dislocation. In the last 18 years I live daily with pain killers. Within a quarter of an hour, I felt an immediate relief. I want to be from now on as near you as possible. I thank you with all my heart. Z.L.

༄

September 2007

I have had diabetes years now. The greatest difficulty was that I had gone blind during the 2nd year in University, in 2001. I was reading using special glasses and from a very small distance, 5 cm from the book. I could not come down the stairs, particularly the white ones, because I could not distinguish the stairs, I could only see a white line. I could only see light; I would bump on my mother and could not see her. On my first meeting with George, 2 o'clock at night, I could see the balcony across the street. On our second meeting I could see the stairs clearly, and on my name day, I discovered I could see colors (I had bought a jumper thinking it was grey, I realized it was green). Today I can see the bus from two blocks away; I can recognize my mother in the street. I do not know whether a person that has his sight intact can understand the feelings of joy, happiness, satisfaction, bliss and independence that overwhelm me with such small, everyday things, but at the same time so important. I cannot find the words to express my gratitude to Mr. George.

With endless love, P.N.

❧

27.1.2007

My son K., on the 6th month after his birth, was found through preventive blood testing to suffer from the thyroid, and we were told to repeat the tests. So we did, and the results showed the index to be higher than normal. A month and a half later we repeated the tests once more, and the levels shown were the same. After Mr. George's help we did the examinations once more and my wife and I were so happy to see the results indicating absolutely normal levels. With no medicine, no doctors. We thank you so much. M.M.

❧

13.6.2005

I want to thank Mr. George for saving my husband. He had lung cancer that made a metastasis to the head. The tumor spread to the entire head. They told us he would last for no more than 6 months. November 2004. Today, seven months later, he is as if he went down with the flu... Th.B.

❧

9.1.2008

My daughter M. could not hear. Today she does, for the first time, and I owe this to Mr. George who cured my child. I thank him so much.

❧

24.7.2008

I came to visit the most beautiful man I've ever known in my life. Mr. George is for me the man who supported me psychologically at the most difficult moment in my life. Nine months ago, going round to all hospitals in Greece and some in America, the doctors kept telling me that my daughter, who had brain cancer which had advanced to hydrocephaly, would die in 10 days, maximum in two months. With Mr. George's help, my daughter is now well, 12 months old, and I am looking forward to her being cured. I thank you so much... E.L.

❧

30.1.2008
Since birth, my leg was atrophic. I could not step on it. I underwent 6 operations. The leg was shorter than the other. With Mr. George's help I can now walk properly. I thank him very much.

❧

14.8.2008
Two months ago we visited Mr. George for the first time, for a problem my husband had (varicocele). Due to his help he is now completely well!!! I am now on my 2nd month pregnant. We thank him from the bottom of our hearts... K.T.

❧

7.11.2005
I had problems with my bones, I was in pain. My

husband had problems with his waist. We did an MRI and the doctor said that he needed an operation. A friend told us about Mr. George and we came to visit him. When we saw him, he inspired confidence to us. What he said was true. The important thing is that we sensed the difference he made before even we left. My husband could sit and stand up with no pain at all. And as Mr. George told us he is going to avoid the operation. We believe in Mr. George, in the help he is giving us, and are looking forward to our next visit to him. We thank you very much. Th.O.

9.12.2005

How can I express my gratitude to Mr. George, who cured my leg today? I could not move my toes, after a serious operation I had. It was divine luck that I came to know a good friend. God help him to give health to people. With love and respect. K.M.

11.12.2005

I could not raise my arm, at all, it had become paralyzed and I could not work, not even cook food for my family. I came to Mr. George and after 2 visits my arm became well again. I had undergone an MRI and the doctors had told me that I would be able to move my arm again only if I had an operation. Fortunately, I heard about Mr. George from a friend. I feel blessed that this man exists and cured me. I thank you ever so much. E.P.

⚜

21.12.2005

My name is G. I came to Mr. George because I could not step on my leg. Mr. George made me well and now I walk properly. Mr. George, I love you so much, I will never forget you. K.L.

⚜

21.12.2005

I had a cyst in the breast, and it disappeared immediately. I could not walk and Mr. George cured my legs, as he did with my waist, my arms, my nerves, my headache and my thyroid. I thank him from the bottom of my heart. O.K.

⚜

17.12.2005

I came with my cousin. What can I say? I am leaving without the meniscus problem that required an operation. I can stretch my leg and bend it with no problem. Thank you very much! E.G.

George, your friends, all of us, G., L., O., thank you for receiving us and helping us. We know what you have done for P, for his leg that he hadn't moved his toes for years, and we pray to God to give you strength. G.,L.,O.

⤞⤝

12.7.2005
Today I had a pain in my arm and a pain in my eye. I was healed in a minute by Mr. George. I wish him well. I am grateful. P.G.

⤞⤝

31.8.2006
With my first visit to Mr. George with a business partner, I saw a great difference in the neck and also – and this is important to me – I was feeling an inner serenity that made me think: 'I wish my business partner doesn't want to leave". He also felt great improvement on his neck and felt the same serenity as I had. When we went to George he had astigmatism and a blurred vision, but when we left he could see perfectly well. From the start I liked George and trusted him from the moment I saw him. I do sincerely believe that he heals people, both psychologically and physically. May he always

be well, to make people well. Sincerely, P.
P.S.
   I also brought my brother, he didn't hear well, and now he does.

⟋⟍⟋⟍

The man with the great gift

My body every moment
Was aching and of pain reminiscent
The doctor's need propped always in mind
In all my movement and of any kind
Shiploads they prescribed of all sorts of pills
Fortunes went their way but left with me all ills
But when dear George was by friends prescribed
Oh, what a lovely man so pure, unbribed,
In Alexandria I ran to find him with zeal and zest
By God this Paschalidis is he trully blessed!!

Here is a man that wins you over with his simplicity. He is joyful, indomitable, cheerful, and above all, endowed with gifts.
   It took one glance and he knew immediately what was wrong with me, and his positive energy, with the help of God, helped me so much. Yes, I can say with certainty that the man performs miracles. George,

your magnificence is above anything, nothing measures against it. Let God keep you well always, bless you and protect you.

I wish to you that for all the good things you offer to people God should repay with His blessings.

With deep respect, a faithful friend of yours. N.M.

~❧~

George, today is the second day I meet you. I am sitting tirelessly next to you for five hours now. Watching you offering light from your light! With such simplicity... I am wondering whether this stoicism of a saint is really the greatest gift God has given to man. You spoke of the one way road that led you to life and to the happiness treading it.

Be well, wherever you are... I thank you that you exist, smiling tirelessly. I consider our meetings an important 'crossroad' in my life and my path of learning. I wish I have more time to be with you.

With love and respect, O.L.

~❧~

5.12.2005

My name is L. I am suffering with ankylosing spondylitis and psoriasis. My friend E. recommended me to George and I came seeking to be helped to become better. Leaving here, I already feel better and I need to look no further. Only God can judge and I thank Him for this gift that George be around helping all of us who were fortunate enough to be in his way. L.T.

I am L's wife. I wish to George to always have such a big embrace to hold us all to his bosom.
    With love, E.T.

❧

21.7.2005
We came today to see Mr. George for my brother's problem of tetraplegia. From the first moment we saw him my brother was able to move his left hand, something impossible until now as he could move nothing at all. About my problem with numbness in the hands and the shoulders: well, in 5 minutes I started to feel differently. We thank Mr. George and we wish him to always be given from God the strength to continue his mission. S.D.
I brought my son to Mr. George because he doesn't speak and to my astonishment, I heard him speak. My persistent headache was also vanished. A big thank you is not enough. May God give him health and strength to keep helping our fellow human beings that have his need.

19.7. 2005

We came as a family today beset with problems: headaches, phobias, gynecological problems, anxieties. We made George's acquaintance for the first time and we thank him for the problems he cleared away. Along with us also came a friend suffering with ankylosing spondylitis and he was cured, so was my mother in law, suffering with gynaecological problems and with her waist. Whatever I write about George is not enough. We thank him and let God keep him well to continue healing all people. S.A.

❧

2.3.2006

My good friend George,

I am one of these fortunate people that came to know you. I feel genuinely happy, because you gave me the opportunity to understand what my unforgettable teacher was telling me, Ms M, a wonderful and rare person who worked so hard for Greece and she loved the entire planet so much. She was a fervent follower of Christ, Whom she loved to the outmost and was teaching His teachings, analyzing and bringing out the depth of His message, in a simple, honest and humble manner. When she was gone, I lost the earth under my feet, and I prayed that I find someone like that enlightened person. My prayers were answered, and in September of 2005, I heard about you from our good friend T.H. My first experience of you was my cure, on the phone. I was suffering from musculoskeletal pain syndrome (fibromyalgia). When I visited you in Alexandria, I was surprised because you diagnosed far more conditions that the tests I had undergone had ever shown (computer tomography, MRI scan), conditions that later were confirmed by ordinary doctors.

The highlights of my experiences were the two miracles that my friends and I experienced together on 1.3.2006 at 11:30 at night, when the phone rang from that mother in Switzerland who informed you that her little girl had started to walk and paint. In the beginning we thought that it was about a young girl that had started doing things. It so happened, though, that the child's grandmother was there who informed us that the girl had problems with her legs and her arms and that the doctors had said there was a need for an operation that would restore things. Yet, after a long operation that lasted 8 hours, again the child could not walk and could not use her right arm. And you cured her by a simple phone call! This was the first shock. The second was after 2 o'clock in the morning, when a woman that was blind since birth saw again! Now I am not surprised on anything, as I am convinced you can do anything, materializing your thought. Thus, you encouraged me to involve myself again with things that benefit man and rejoice in the knowledge which so artfully routine and the pettiness of people take us away from and disorientate us. For, most of the people ignore the saying of Christ that "you are gods", with the result that we leave ourselves exposed to the tempests and the vicissitudes of life. Yet, as the laws of nature are made for man and not man for them, let us wake up in us the small god, and then the darkness will lift and the sun will shine of knowledge, love and happiness.

I thank you so much! Ch.TH.

❧

August 2009

I hold that God was very generous with me, when He sent to me Mr. Paschalidis, right at the moment when I needed him.

Through his help and guidance the problem of malignancy I had was reduced and cleared in the best way and the medical tests I took subsequently had showed very good results.

But the point I want to ponder on is not the help he so generously gives, to all that may ask, at the physical, bodily level. In my eyes, the greatest help he gives, that most psychotherapists would envy, is none other than the brief, in depth and accurate outline of the self he performs to all, explaining to him or her roots of the problem and helping him or her, through the redirection of energy, to change it.

A psychotherapy express, based on happiness, I could call it.

And all this he gives within an immense, unconditional love and in such a way that this becomes a lesson of life to all of us.

I cannot forget the endless love that I feel next to him, and his exhortation: "I do now want you to always be next to me. I want you to become well, to be happy, to smile, to enjoy life and not to need me. I am just the ramp that helps you stretch your wings and fly".

I want, Mr. George, to thank you from the depths of my heart for all that you give to us and teach us, and I pray to God to give you strength to continue the work you are doing, because it is valuable and we need it.

E.A.

June 2009

Our dearest Mr. George

I am expressing in this way what I feel and comes up to me when I listen to you narrating to us and explaining in such a simple and intelligible way, but I could never say it in public... (I remain, it seems, a B type)! I would like first of all to see to it that you feel the admiration I nurture for your gift that you so generously share with us and, secondly, the gratitude I feel that you do not desert us, even if we have done it first.

My admiration also turns to your dear wife, Mrs. Chrysoula, because I deem admirable her sacrifice so that we all can reap the benefits of you.

I compare her with me, that for so many times, when my husband was travelling for his job – our only source of income – I was complaining and making his life difficult, and almost always, he would depart for his trips sour and after a fight.... 'I did it out of love because I would miss him." I may have told you, then. I should have knwn better."

I am wondering now that my husband suffers with cancer and has such a hard time with chemotherapies for a second time in his life how much I and my attitude may have contributed to this, as he did complain very often "you have bloated me". But I would continue on my own theme for whatever topic may then have come up.

Now that I am scared I may lose him; that I have to go through the insecurity of the therapy, that he is always by me because he cannot cope with the travels in his job, you are my only hope, my only source of faith that things will go well.

How many times have I now wished that time could roll back, that I had not made the mistakes I made, how often have I wished that we had come across you sooner and that we knew then what we know today. Blessed are those who come to know you early enough! I am sending you my humble thanks for all that you have done for us today, and I am praying that God would bless you and give you the strength to put up with us people... our wonderful Mr. George... D.S.